*Illuminating His World,
His Purpose, and His Plan*

REIGNITING
THE KINGDOM
OF GOD

DR. PAULA R. GARNER

Copyright © 2024 - Dr. Paula Garner
All rights reserved.

Unless otherwise indicated all scripture quotations are taken from the KING JAMES VERSION of the Bible. Public Domain. Scripture quotations marked (Amp) are taken from the AMPLIFIED® BIBLE, Copyright © 1954, 1958, 1962, 1964, 1965, 1987 by the Lockman Foundation Used by Permission. (www.Lockman.org). Scripture quotations marked (NRSV) are taken from the NEW REVISED STANDARD VERSION BIBLE, copyright © 1989 the Division of Christian Education of the National Council of the Churches of Christ in the United States of America. Used by permission. All rights reserved. Scripture quotations marked (ESV) are taken from THE HOLY BIBLE, ENGLISH STANDARD VERSION®, Copyright © 2001 by Crossway, a publishing ministry of Good News Publishers. Used by permission. No part of this publication may be reproduced, distributed, transmitted in any form or by any means, including photocopying, recording, or other electronic or mechanical methods, without the prior written permission of the author, except in the case of brief quotations embodied in critical reviews and certain other noncommercial uses permitted by copyright law. For permission requests, contact the author at the email below.

REIGNITING THE KINGDOM OF GOD
Illuminating His World, His Purpose, and His Plan

ISBN #978-1-943342-52-5

Dr. Paula R. Garner
Cedar Rapids, Iowa
swicm@cfaith.com

Printed in the United States of America
Destined To Publish
www.destinedtopublish.com

DEDICATION

I dedicate this book to Jesus for using me to bring this message. I also dedicate this book to my son, Nathan, my grandchildren, Quinton and Emery, and to all those who, like me, are life learners and truth seekers who will relentlessly pursue His kingdom and His righteousness. Lastly, to all the multitudes who are in the valley of decision, Joel 3:14.

Acknowledgments

Thank you, Apostle Carolyn Wallace, for believing and bringing out the best of me in Christ. Thank you, Marilyn and the Destined to Publish team, Coach Kara and Deborah; without your guidance and expertise, we would not be in print. Thank you to all those who prayed for me and endured with me through getting to publication of this book (you know who you are)!

Contents

Introduction: The Invisible King and His Kingdom 1
   Falling in love with the captor 4
   The kingdom revealed 6
Part I: HIS WORLD – God as Creator 11
  Chapter 1: How We Perceive 13
   Impact of one's perspective 13
   The estate planner 17
   His assets 19
  Chapter 2: Where Ideas Come From 23
   Precepts and concepts 24
   How to use precepts 26
   How to understand His precepts 27
  Chapter 3: Precepts Are Found Through Study 31
   Satan's rise and fall 38
   Spiritual Stockholm Syndrome: How the light dims . . 41
   The sovereignty of God 48
   The authority of the Creator 49
   God shows us proof of His authority 50

    The lesson of submission 51
Part II: HIS PURPOSE – Jesus 53
  Chapter 4: Understanding God's Purpose 55
    Appreciating God's purpose 56
    God's blueprint. 63
    Man's desires 67
    John the Baptist challenges the old school 72
    Are we, too, missing His message? 74
  Chapter 5: The Gospel 76
    The two roles of Jesus 78
    Jesus' message: the gospel of the kingdom 80
    How we're getting it wrong today 84
    Becoming kingdom minded 86

Part III: HIS PLAN – The Holy Spirit 91
  Chapter 6: God's Renovation Plan for Man 93
    Jesus' enlightenment of Nicodemus 95
    Work out your soul salvation. 97
    Who is the Holy Spirit? 101
  Chapter 7: Changing citizenship 104
    The desire to change 104
    Recredentialling 106
    The application. 108
    Passing the test. 108
    Finding a sponsor 115
    Medical examination. 116
  Chapter 8: Power for the future. 118
    Being in and not immersed 118
    From promise to power. 119
    Heavenly messaging 122

    Our spiritual enablement. 124
    Ambassadors 128

Conclusion: Becoming a Citizen of the Kingdom 131

Appendix **139**

I.   Scriptures supporting things that were completed in God's eternal world BEFORE the earth was created. Knowing these scriptures and looking up the definitions of the highlighted words will change your perspective on how you read the bible. 139

II.   Scriptures that support man's captivity, i.e. under Satan's rule, the kingdom of darkness, i.e. (Spiritual Stockholm Syndrome) 143

III. Scriptures supporting the importance God placed on children. The important factor here is that there is no extension of his kingdom if there are no offspring. . 144

IV. Scriptures supporting the prophets speaking of the coming of the kingdom of God 145

V.   Scriptures supporting Jesus preaching the gospel of the kingdom of God 146

VI. Scriptures supporting the Apostles expansion of the preaching of the gospel of the kingdom 146

VII. Scriptural support that the baptism of the Holy Spirit with the evidence of speaking in tongues was the power given to the Apostles which they received in the upper room and extended to those who were baptised as they spread the gospel of the kingdom to the Jews and Gentiles. 148

VIII. Scriptures supporting the importance of God's precepts, His commands/laws that govern His kingdom. These are not the ritual laws of the Old Testament but His governing principles that rule over His kingdom that King David wrote about which made him a man after God's own heart. 152

INTRODUCTION

The Invisible King and His Kingdom

There once was a King of an invisible, faraway country. This King is a one of a kind being that he transcends time, space and matter. There was nothing before him or ever will be like him. As one self-sustaining eternal being, the king, can transform himself into three distinct persons, one as a father, creator of all life, two, as a son, an heir to the throne and lastly as a agent, assigned to enforce the King's plan. They are called the trinity, and they are the responsible parties that crafted, designed, and fulfil all life in the kings country. The remaining part of the King's world is comprised of a staff; an army of celestial being, with a hierarchical structure and roles adhering to governing laws and principles that the King has set in place. These governing principles and laws are a function of the eternal fabric of the Ks country and will never be changed

Introduction

However, there was an uprising in the kingdom where one of the King's closest staff members attempted a coup to unseat the King. Upon the realization of this attempt, the King immediately dealt with the staff member and those who were swept from the kingdom by him. The King stripped the staff member of all his authority and the power he had been granted, and then banished all of them from his kingdom, as his crimes were unforgivable. They were now known as enemies of the state, exiled for eternity from the countries headquarter location.

Prior to this assault against the invisible kingdom, the Kpulled together his trinity and they discussed their desire to duplicate their invisible kingdom into another realm in a faraway country. They all talked thoroughly through the plan and considered every contingency that would be needed for the plan to be fulfilled. To fool proof the plan, the King appointed his son to house his creation in his spiritual womb until the appointed time to release them into the earth. This allowed the son to infuse the future creation with the kingdoms DNA, giving them his indelible markers, of his identity within them. He also delegated his enforcer to ensure the unity and integrity of the trinity would be operable and accessible in man to aid him in completing his future assignments.

Now, the King decided to put his words into action and created a physical universe filled with planets and galaxies, one of which he would make habitable for his sons' offspring. He called that planet Earth. He formed his prototype, a man, that they had conceived in his invisible realm and placed him in the earth and breathed his breath of life into him. This man would now have the creative ability of the King, the DNA of the son and the power

Introduction

of the enforcer to become the Kings representatives in the new earth. He would be endowed with dominion and authority for the purpose of reproducing and duplicating the operation of the Kings invisible kingdom on the new earth.

Now the King walked and talked with the man and gave him responsibilities and one command to adhere to. They had a pure and unobstructed relationship; they were as one. Now to complete the Kings earthly plan, he made a woman from a part of the man to promulgate his plan for them in the earth. They would multiply by populating the new earth with the species of God, taking their delegated authority to carry out replicating the Kings world, purpose, and plan in the earth.

As the man was developing his relationship with the King, he broke the one command he had been given by entertaining a foreign voice. That voice was the former staff member, who had been cast out the invisible kingdom but not destroyed. He had been stalking the actions of the King from a distance. He watched how the King gave the man authority to rule in this new earth, so he decided to make another attempt against the King by coming after his offspring. He stepped out of the darkness and entered the physical earth realm. He gained the permission of a serpent to enter his body and began a conversation with the woman to deceive them. This was the second time the former staff member, now a stalker turned kidnapper, had attempted to overthrow the government of the King. This time, he was successful at obtaining the man and woman's allegiance, thus setting off a catastrophic chain of events for the man.

Because of the man's choice not to keep the king's command, the king had to withdraw His enforcer from the man and force

INTRODUCTION

the man out of his garden. The man had severed his connection with the King and had become a hostage of the stalker. The man knew something had changed but did not truly grasp the entirety of the new kingdom he was now a part of. By stealing humanity from the womb of the King, man would be blinded by his true biological identity. Now the kidnapper could raise the man and his offspring. Humanity would now be destined to a life of labor and suffering with no hope, no future, and no ability to know their true ing—or so the kidnapper thought.

Falling in love with the captor

Now the man, being captive to his kidnapper, was disconnected from his home with no natural way of finding his way back to his original kingdom. He and the woman had no other recourse but to move forward with their life. All they knew at this point was that they no longer walked and talked with the King, so the man and his wife adjusted and embraced the behaviours and culture of their new kingdom of darkness as directed by their captor. In today's society, we would call this Stockholm Syndrome. I will talk more about this in a later chapter.

Immediately, the King announced his recovery plan for the man, that he had devised from the beginning as he knew that giving the man free will had the potential to evolve into this situation. With haste, the King decreed to send his first-born son, his heir to get his man back and restore his kingdom. So, the royal son left his father's kingdom to find the man. The royal son went so far as to strip himself from his status in his father's invisible kingdom and went down to the far country where the man was. He knew just where to find the man and found him

INTRODUCTION

fishing on the sea. He asked the man, "Have you caught any fish?" and the man said no and pulled his boat into the shore. Then the son asked him, "How did you get here?" The man said, "What do you mean? I was born in this country, along with all the others you see around me. Our population keeps growing every day." The man further stated, "In our country, we must make our own living, get our own food and water, and provide our own shelter. Everything we need we must work for. It's hard, but we all have become used to it. So who are you?"

The royal son said, "I am from a royal family, from another faraway kingdom, and I have come to tell you that this country is not the country of your birth. This is not where you are from! You are an heir to the throne of the kingdom I am from, and I have come to find you and reunite you with your real royal family." The man said, "This place is all I have known, why do you say that?" The royal son said, "You were taken hostage from our family long before you can remember. Your captor did not request a ransom for you; rather, he kidnapped you and took you for his own and raised you up under his kingdom. Because of your blindness or lack of knowledge of the past event, you have no idea that your identity has been hijacked. Our father has sent me to find you and tell you that you are of royal descent and to free you from your captor. Our DNA matches. We are of the same bloodline, which makes us inheritors of his kingdom. Even though your captor did not ask for a ransom, I know what it will take and will pay the penalty required to free you from his bondage. I hope you see how much you mean to me."

The son continued, "In our country, you have royal status. You have access to everything our King has. You will never want for anything, and he will always be by your side." The man said, "How can this be? My current situation isn't so bad. I have a way to make a living, I am used to navigating around the wars, mistreatment, anger, drunkenness, reckless behaviors, and manipulations that others are constantly involved in. I help anyone who is in trouble or has a need as much as I can. Furthermore, there are also other good people like me who will do anything to help me when I need it. I am not sure why I need to be a part of this royal family you speak of." The royal son said, "I know this is hard for you to understand. However, I promise you that when you choose to join me in our home kingdom, you will see that what I am telling you is true. You will see that you are of the same image and likeness of our father, but you must choose to come with me, I will not take you hostage or force you. I am telling you the truth, but you have to trust me."

The kingdom revealed

So the man chose to leave with the royal son to this new kingdom. As the man was departing from his old country, he met with a lot of opposition from his current family. They said he was crazy and foolish to follow someone to a place he had never been before. They pleaded with him and tried to stop him, but they were unsuccessful because he had made up his mind.

When the man and the royal son arrived in the new kingdom, the man was amazed. His initial introduction to the kingdom was overwhelming, and he felt immediately at peace. He did not see any poor or destitute people. He did not see fighting, arguments, or wars among the people. He saw that all the people who accepted and lived in this kingdom had everything in common,

Introduction

including their wealth. There was no lack seen at all. So the man asked the royal son, "When do we go fishing to get dinner?" And the royal son said to him, "You don't have to work to get it, it's already provided for us. Just ask the King using my name, and I will get you what you need. This is how we operate in our King's kingdom." Then the man said, "I left everything and brought nothing with me. I only have the clothes on my back, so what will I do for clothing?" The royal son responded, "You don't have to worry about that either; our King will take care of it."

Lastly, the man requested something to drink, and the royal son called for someone to bring him as much water as he needed and replied, "All of this is already provided for you. All you must do is learn to adapt to your new kingdom by seeking and adhering to the kingdom's operation. By your willful acknowledgment to join me in this kingdom, you now have rights and privileges as a citizen with official immigration papers to obtain full access to all it has to offer. There are many benefits yet for you to discover that cannot be exhausted in one day. I know it is overwhelming, but it will soon be your natural way of life. You will see that this kingdom is run by faith in our King and not by your works."

The royal son explained to the man, "Our King's plan was for me to pay the ransom required to get you back so you would again be with him when I present you to him as a citizen of his Kdom. All of this is to reintroduce you to the life that you once had and were not aware of because your captor stole your identity illegally and made it his own. You are now a joint heir of the invisible kingdom along with me. Now my assignment is completed here on earth. I must go back to our king and will not be with you physically any longer. However, I am leaving you my name, as it will be the key

Introduction

to accessing the King and his kingdom benefits. He has put my name above every other name in creation for you and the others who will follow so you can invoke his power and presence in your earthly circumstances. Lastly, he has provided you with his Enforcer, who will be beside you, just as I am present with you, to be your personal guide to teach and answer all questions you have about the kingdom. He will show you what the king likes and dislikes and how to use diplomacy to impact relations with others in the earth. He will show you how to speak the language of your home country, how it operates, how to love others, and how to be in right alignment with our government, and he will be your comforter in all times of trouble.

When you fully embrace him, he will show you how to wield the power he invested in you to defeat every enemy that comes against you, even your own mind. All of this is freely given to you, so you can navigate freely, knowing you are fully covered and secured by the King's government. Don't allow your past to haunt you. You are now in a protected status and accountable to his principles. Our King has a host of staff in his realm that he has made available to you for your protection, and nothing by any means will harm you. This is our father's promise. Additionally, please know that receiving his citizenship is just the beginning: you have been given an assignment to fulfil now. The King's enforcer will be responsible for helping you in that process, but you must work together with him, as everything he speaks comes directly from me and the King, for we are all one. Do not fear or think you must earn this. It has been freely given to you as a citizen of his kingdom for all eternity. Your job is to learn its operation and fulfil your purpose in carrying out his plan in the earth."

Introduction

This allegory in its entirety is the sum of God's world, His purpose, and His plan for humanity which we have in the Bible. Here, God is represented as the King, creator of everything. Jesus is the Son the heir who came to earth to recover His children. Man is represented as God's creation. The Holy Spirit is represented as the God's enforcer, who oversees commissioning God's power to guide, teach, lead, and restore the Kings's citizens back to their true identify and governing authority. Lastly, Satan is represented as the stalker, hostage taker, kidnapper who is the enemy of the state in the earth.

Please note that I am not attempting to be God, nor saying that I have exhausted every answer one could possibly have, as I am a mere creature and not the Creator. However, as I read the entirety of the scriptures, God's original plan is clearly the extension and establishment of His heavenly kingdom on the earth through His creation. He extended himself in the form of His Son and His Spirit into the earth realm to defend, protect, and preserve His posterity. Walk with me as we revisit the scriptures from His perspective, in terms of His purpose and plan. Once we understand His purpose and plan, it will assuredly pave the way to bring more revelation to our individual purpose and the aggregate purpose of man in the earth.

The answers of life are found in God's big picture of life. God wired us to desire the big picture. That is why we were given an intellect: to reason, to thoughtfully consider His perspective as it pertains to the life he created for man. Not to develop our own perspective, but rather for us to gain His perspective as the author of the Bible. Very simplistically speaking, the big picture of God is found in Genesis chapters 1 and 2. There we find His

Introduction

big picture, His desire to extend His kingdom to earth by way of His offspring ruling and reigning with their delegated authority. The remaining chapters are all about His restoration process to get His offspring back from their free will choice in the garden. God is committed to His world, His plan, and His purpose, and we must position ourselves to be in alignment with Him. The caveat is, we must relinquish our own selfish ambition and seek His kingdom to get there. The following pages tell His story about His world, His purpose and His plan.

Part I:

His World – God as Creator

CHAPTER 1
How We Perceive

If you are anything like me, sometimes when you read a book, you skip over the introduction, preface, or foreword to get to the heart of the book. If you are one of those people, I urge you to go back and read the introduction first before you proceed.

Impact of one's perspective

Perspective is everything. The vantage point from which we view something has a serious impact on our perception. We get our perspective from our and others' experiences, ideas, debates, historical events, analysis, and the list goes on. Our posture, position, and attitude play an important role in our ability to perceive correctly. We all bring our own truth to the table of opinions. If our posture, position, and attitude is one of doubt, disbelief, or scepticism to any concept, then our perspective won't change.

I remember taking my son to our first professional baseball game at the White Sox stadium in Chicago. His baseball training camp team had tickets for all the participants and their families. This was not just an event for me, because I played softball throughout college and loved baseball. So we went with great expectation of being in the atmosphere with other fans, and of course the game. As we entered the stadium, I pulled out our tickets and saw that we were in row 12, section 500. I was like, "Wow, these will be great seats, row 12." Little did we know that the row number did not mean a good seat, it was the section number that determined our vantage point. As we continued to climb the steep stairs up and up, I realized that our view was not going to be great at all. When we sat down, we could not distinguish the players and could hardly read their numbers. I mean, how was I going to see Frank "The Big Hurt" Thomas up close? But that was not going to happen. I chalked that experience up as a wash and made up my mind that I never had to go to another professional baseball game again. It was not a bad experience, rather, it was too much travel time, expense, and walking just to get a seat that was worse than watching from a monitor. I would have been better off in my own home, with my cheap snacks, comfortable couch, and controlled climate with a perfect view.

That all changed when I received an invitation to attend another game at the same stadium. My first inclination was to reject the invitation because I had already "been there, done that." However, my friend insisted that I go again so I could experience it from a

How We Perceive

different perspective. This time I had been given Corporate Sky Box seats. Still unimpressed, due to my last experience, but I said to myself, "It might be nice, but I don't think it is going to change my perspective and be worth all that time again," Nevertheless, I said yes. My goodness, this was a whole different vibe from my first experience of walking in the parking lot of 7,000 spaces and traveling up Lord knows how many steep stairs, just to not have an acceptable view of the game. This time when I went in, I was directed to go to a special parking area close to the building for Sky Box attendees. Additionally, there was an elevator to get to the floor my seat was on. The box seat was in an air-conditioned private unit, and the food was top notch and endless. I had no idea that this type of experience was available. I was at the same field, watching the same players, and yet, because I accepted the invitation to go back and experience it from another vantage point, it opened up a whole new world for me and my perspective made a tremendous shift.

You may say, "Well, duh, who doesn't know about Sky Box tickets and the amenities they have?" Well, I was not aware. No one among my friends and family had ever had this experience that I had just been made aware of, so it was new to me. We make assumptions that everyone is knowledgeable about the simple things, but that is not true, as we only know what we have been exposed to until we find that there is more to know in that same experience. This holds true concerning the Bible as well. One would assume that all Christians read the Bible, but what I have found is that we do more listening than actual personal reading and study. Moreover, when we do actually study, we often study to support what we already know. Whether you are a believer in

Jesus or not, do not do a disservice to yourself by failing to revisit what you think you already understand. There might just be a hidden elevator and a closer parking space that leads you to a dimension of your experience that enlightens your understanding of the kingdom of God. He has the ultimate Sky Box seat from which we are able to sit at His feet and experience and see more than we would ever be able to do on our own.

If I had stuck with my perspective from the first game sitting in the nosebleed section and declined the second invitation, I would have missed knowing there was a much better way to experience the game. I also realized that it would be more expensive to continue to get those kinds of seats, but if that is what gave me the best experience, it would be worth it every time. It was not the actual box seat that changed my mind, but knowing that I had access to the seat changed the game for me.

It costs to seek, to search, to pursue understanding. The question we have to ask is, are we willing to open ourselves up to a new perspective, or will we remain satisfied with what we think we know? I'm saying this to demonstrate that often the way we are introduced to something can leave an everlasting impression. However, we must remain open to see the same situation from another perspective and get a better understanding before we make a final determination or assessment of its value. In doing so, we may find that the things we once held sacred and received as facts will now have to bow before the truth. Being amenable is the key to get to true understanding. As the Bible says in Proverbs 4:4-7,

> *He taught me also, and said unto me, Let thine heart retain my words: keep my commandments, and live. Get*

wisdom, get understanding: forget it not; neither decline from the words of my mouth. Forsake her not, and she shall preserve thee: love her, and she shall keep thee. Wisdom is the principal thing; therefore get wisdom: and with all thy getting get understanding.

The estate planner

Another example of a perspective would be to view God as an estate planner. The definition of an estate planner is someone engaged in "the preparation of tasks that serve to manage the owners asset base"[1] to ensure its inheritors are the recipients of the estate as deemed by the planner. This was all explained in Genesis 1:26-28.

> *And God said, Let us make man in our image, after our likeness: and let them have dominion over the fish of the sea, and over the fowl of the air, and over the cattle, and over all the earth, and over every creeping thing that creepeth upon the earth. So God created man in his own image, in the image of God created he him; male and female created he them. And God blessed them, and God said unto them, Be fruitful, and multiply, and replenish the earth, and subdue it: and have dominion over the fish of the sea, and over the fowl of the air, and over every living thing. that moveth upon the earth.*

Everything that He owns he calls His kingdom. A great man of God, Dr. Myles Munroe, cited the best definition of the kingdom of God, stating, "The kingdom of God is the governing influence of a king over his territory impacting it with his personal will, purpose, and intent producing a culture with values, morals and a life style that reflects the kings desires and nature for his citizens." That being said, and in alignment with scripture, we can visualize God as the master estate planner.

Let's look at what makes Him a master estate planner. He must have assets: an extensive area of land (the universe) that has a landowner (Haggai 2:8; Psalm 24:1, 50:10-12, 115:16; Colossians 1:17; 1 Peter 4:10). The planning includes the settlement (to give or leave by will or the handing down) of assets to one's heirs. Most estate plans require a lawyer with an expertise in estate law. (1 John 2:1). Wills are another aspect of one's estate plan. They deal with the payout of the assets at one's death (John 14:25) and also include other directives like power of attorney, health care decisions, and beneficiaries, as well as naming the testator, guardian, and executor (1 Timothy 2:5, Hebrews 9:15), all of which He fulfils.

All throughout the Bible, there are records of historical events, but it does not always explain how they happened. As humans, we can only fill in the unexplainable gaps with our limited knowledge or dismiss the event as false. However, God has left clues within His words in the Bible that will lead us to more answers. As we read the scriptures, it will become apparent that He continually reveals Himself by rolling back the curtain of eternity to give His citizens insight into His mind for the fulfilment of His purposes. Deuteronomy 29:29 says it clearly:

How We Perceive

The secret things belong unto the LORD our God: but those things which are revealed belong unto us and to our children for ever, that we may do all the words of this law.

To understand this revelation of His kingdom, we must see it from His perspective as the master estate planner of the world He created. The idea here is that God preplanned His estate in His mind. In His wisdom, He pre-solved every possibility, dotted every "i," and crossed every "t" before he gave it physical formation with his words. As much as we may want to question His decisions, or question any other creator's decision about why they made a product, the answers will always remain with their will and purpose. We can alter the product if we choose, but that will never negate the intentions of the creator's original purpose. We will explore this later when we discuss what He did before the foundation of the world.

His assets

Let's evaluate where the estate planner got his assets from. If I were to ask you, "When did your life start?" what would you say? Most of us would respond with the day we were born. Others would say it started when their parent(s) found out they were pregnant. I submit to you that although those responses are plausible, neither of those answers is the truth. We see our existence as starting out as an idea in our parent's mind to bring forth a child into the earth. From that idea, a plan for our life was formulated by them. Their idea was not just to have a boy or a girl, it was to provide and prepare for life—a life that would demonstrate their love and affection toward you by putting their plans into action.

Their planning included providing the right nutrients to help you develop in the womb, taking proper vitamins, etc., figuring out how they would get to the hospital when labour starts, and preparing your room with all the things you would need to be cared for properly. Nurturing you to navigate the world in terms of how to eat, love, give, walk, talk and behave. Showing you that if you followed their instructions, nothing would be impossible for you to accomplish, and they would do all they could to protect you.

After all that, wisdom advised your parents to create a plan that would cover how they would respond if you chose to become disobedient. They knew that since you would be born with free will, you would have the ability to choose not to follow their instruction. It was never their intention for you to choose to follow instructions from a voice other than theirs. But your free will automatically offered a threat to the life's plan they had prepared. The thought of your intentional rebellion or requesting emancipation from them never entered their mind.

So, a deterrent had to be put into place: a disciplinary plan that would be severe enough to keep you on the path and plan they established. They did not inform you of this plan, as it would only go into effect based on your choices. This idea of inflicting punishment was not made from anger but out of love (Proverbs 16:4). Free will has consequences, and we will talk about this more in later chapters; however, we must know that when we don't choose, we are still choosing, and the impacts of those non-choices will become evident.

The ideas in your parents' imagination had now been resolved and their approach agreed upon. Now it was time to implement the plan: your parents announced their intentions to bring the actual physical life forth and they committed to an act that they do not control to bring you in the earth. They did not know the day of conception, birth, gender or death. The parallel here is that as much as we want to believe we are in control of life, we never have controlled the process of our being. We did not just arrive in this world by accident, regardless of what you were told or may think regarding the circumstances of your birth. Our parents were just the vehicle God used to bring us into the earth. Scripture tells us how we got here as much thought went into God's preparing for humanity's existence.

In His perfect world humanity started out as His plan. He preplanned our existence before there was an earth (Eph 1:4). He gave us purpose (Gen 1:26). He built in the procreative process into mankind (Gen 1:28). He built a planet for us (Gen 1). Lastly, He gave us a physical body and placed us amid all His creation to take dominion over it (Gen 2:7). We were destined in the earth by His will and for His purpose. Demonstrating more of His expertise in estate planning! This is the set up for the framework of His world, His purpose, and His plan, which started from eternity and ends in eternity.

In summary, we have outlined God as master estate planner and visualized His perspective like that of newlyweds planning for their family. Now that I have given you a conceptualization of His plan, we can take those mental images as a part of the big picture of His world. This will frame our ideology, which will impact our theology and philosophy infiltrating our mentality and attitude toward the kingdom of God. We cannot go into His realm with our own ideas. Everything must be driven from His perspective if our goal is to be accurate in our assessment of His construction of our lives. Honestly, to say that we can reconstruct His world and plan would be like a baby coming out of its mother's womb and telling her how and why they came into existence while advising her of the plan they have for their own life. It is imperative that we approach seeing God from heaven's perspective to earth, and not from an earthly perspective to heaven.

CHAPTER 2

WHERE IDEAS COME FROM

For me or anyone else to write a book, there must first come an idea. Ideas are powerful, as they can outlive a person. Ideas come from things that already exist. There is no original thought. Solomon told us that there is nothing new under the sun (Ecclesiastes 1:9). For example, by definition, the first tsunami was when God parted the Red Sea, the first satellite was heaven, the first airplanes were angels, the first light was Jesus, the first telegraph was prayer, the first tablet was the law the Moses brought down from Mt Saini and the list goes on. Everything started in heaven. All man has done is augment, reinvent, redesign, reexplore, repurpose, redevelop, reengineer, resurface, reconstruct, and rename thoughts that came out of heaven into the earth. Since the beginning of time, everything that has been or will be invented, designed, revealed, developed, or engineered is made from what man has extracted and formulated from the earth obtaining the idea from heaven. I am not devaluing man's ingenuity, but rather placing it within its proper context. It was a part of the creativity God put into all mankind from the beginning. You ask, "How so?" The Apostle Paul told us in 1 Corinthians 2:16 that we have the mind of Christ. The mind He gave us was not to instruct Him but to be instructed by Him. So, how can we know God's mind? Where did it begin?

Precepts and concepts

God says to put line upon line and precept upon precept (Isaiah 28:10). Today, we don't use the term precept very often; we talk in terms of concepts. Concepts are a formulation of ideas that come together to create physical or mental images. In God's world, His concepts come from His precepts. So, what are precepts?

The word precept means "any commandment or order intended as an authoritative rule of action; but applied particularly to commands respecting moral conduct [2]", an example would be the 10 commandments. Those 10 precepts are the foundation for ethical living that came from heaven to earth by the hand of God. Another precept is found in God's intent for gender assignment, i.e. male and female. There are no other commandments that proceeded these. Another way to think about it is like the saying before I can redefine any concept or alter a doctrine in the bible, I must find it's original precept to determine God's stance to endure that we get to the core or root of how things were intended. This is very valuable as it ensures that one does not get off course from the original thought. Nevertheless, God established precepts, His original thoughts about His kingdom, what He desired, purposed, and planned, and He had them written in the scriptures so that we would not build new precepts or thoughts that would lead us down the wrong path. In 1 Corinthians 10-11, the Apostle Paul tells us that we need to take heed how we build on God's foundation that is Jesus Christ. We know that if the building will last, we have to start with the proper foundation.

I will dive further into this later, but let me give you an example of how not knowing a precept can be misleading. I had a friend who told me a story one day about how in elementary school during the holiday season, the school had come up with a concept of having a "Food Drive." This "Food Drive" would constitute of the children going home and bringing back donations of non-expired canned and or dry food to give out to families that would be put in boxes and handed out to low-income or needy families, as they were called during those days. Thinking this was a great thing to do for the community so he joyfully helped to pack the boxes and took pride in being able to participate in bringing joy to another family's life.

After the drive was over now it was time for the school administrators picked up the boxes to be distributed a few days prior to the holiday. Anxious for the holiday vacation from school on the last day as he was walking home, he came up to the porch of his house and noticed the familiar box from school. He was startled at why this box was on his porch, and he took it into the house and said to his mom, "Where did you get this box from?" She said, "I did not see it, it must have been donated to us." They opened up the box, and lo and behold, it was one of the boxes of food that he had prepared at school. He turned and looked at his mom and said, "Mom, are we poor?"

What he did not know was the definition of "poor." From his perspective, he and his siblings had everything they needed—food, clothes, shelter—so why would they be considered poor? What he was unaware of was that poverty was defined by the government with some sort of metric that calculated household income and the number of individuals who lived within the household. If a family or individual met those guidelines, then they were entitled to receive certain benefits. Not knowing the precept of poverty created by his government, he was ignorant of its impact on his life. Hence, precepts are important to our understanding of why things are.

How to use precepts

So, how does this relate to the Bible? It shows us the importance of precepts and how they set the stage for the development of our thinking. God knows that everything begins and ends with our mind, renewed or unrenewed. When new information comes into our mind, it looks for a file in our brain to see if it has previous information and/or experience. If an experience or file is found, without further or deeper investigation, we launch our conclusions from that platform, right or wrong. If we do not find a file, we either research the information or, most often, we make a snap judgment based on our best thinking. This can lead to great error and deception because, as finite beings, we have not experienced, read, or had personal involvement or expertise with all things concerning life in or out of this planet.

Therefore, if our concepts and imagery of God's world are not filtered through His established precepts, then our entire understanding of His world, purpose, and plan are off course. As citizens of His kingdom, we can no longer afford to be ignorant of God's plan, as He has already spoken His precepts in the scriptures. Scripture says in 1 John 5:19 (AMP), *"we know [for a fact] that we are of God, and the whole world [around us] lies in the power of the evil one [opposing God and his precepts]."*

Our job is to trust that what He has spoken is the truth and not to be changed or challenged by our own best thinking. Knowing His truth does not have an expiration date. God's words never become old fashioned or out of date. Why? Because He is the originator of it all. As the scriptures say in Romans 3:4, *"…let God be true but every man a liar…"*

How to understand His precepts

So, we have read that it is of the utmost importance to hold true to the precepts or original ideas He has set forth so we can accurately interpret two things, first, His role, and second, our role in His kingdom. Not understanding His precepts is like looking at a one-dimensional picture of the highest peak of Mt. Everest and thinking that picture represents the entire mountain range. Since we believe He is the Creator and ruler of all things, we must step out of our finite understanding and into His mind through His lenses, which are spiritual and not natural. We must allow the Holy Spirit to lead us into understanding God's kingdom and His motivation for human life. We did not precede Him, He preceded us. No matter who we are, we are influenced by the culture in which we were raised or currently live in, therefore our context of a given philosophy will be dominated by those experiences.

If you have ever experienced living in a different culture, you know that everything you do does not necessarily translate from one culture or country to another. You find that some things are permissible in the new culture or country that would never be tolerated, and vice versa. Therefore, to live and communicate correctly in a new culture, the precepts of that culture cannot be ignored—one must become immersed in it. As the scripture says, you must be born again to enter and see the kingdom of God, but we will get into that later. If they drive on the left-hand side of the road in your new culture and your experience has been with driving on the right-hand side, then you will have to adjust and relearn the mechanics from their perspective. You don't get to drive on the right-hand side because it is more comfortable for you. We must adapt, otherwise we will be breaking the law and/or causing an accident, potentially putting ourselves and others' lives in danger, or in jail all because of our unwillingness to adjust.

In God's realm, His kingdom, He has an established operation. His realm is not a bunch of thunderclouds where He sits on a throne judging and zapping us every day for our sin. It's a realm that has functionality, hierarchy, roles and positions, and celestial creatures who carry out, support and are governed by His world. The inability to physically see His realm does not make it unreal or less true, but it is by our faith we know it to be. For some, this is hard to fathom, as our nature is to believe what we can see and doubt what we cannot.

Again, to understand His precepts, we must go back to Genesis chapters 1-2. That is where He clearly states His intentions, as it is the foundation of what He desired in creating mankind. If we don't understand His precept of extending the operation of His heavenly kingdom to earth (Matthew 6:10) through mankind, then we have missed the foundation of what God was trying to establish. The United Kingdom's monarchical government is closely related to how the operation in heaven is like. In their country, they have a king or queen, who is in the position as the sovereign (divine ruler) of the country's government. They have absolute authority over the colonies they have conquered. Once they have conquered a territory, they have a governor who is handpicked by the king and sent to the colony to establish and transform it into the image and likeness of the home country. When the king visits the territory, he has a protocol to be followed that includes an official communication sent by a herald to the colony long in advance of the king's arrival to announce his coming. The king's position can only be inherited by his firstborn offspring. The crown jewels are owned by the government and never belong to the sitting king or queen; they belong to the sovereign's nation. If and/or when a colony rejects the rule of the sovereign country and sets up another form of government, then the governor must leave the territory. These operating principles align with the biblical references to the government of God that is established in the scriptures.

Notwithstanding, there are still some supernatural precepts that we will never fully understand unless God reveals them. For example, medical science cannot figure out how to create a sperm or egg, nor how an egg unites with the sperm to create a human. They do not know the actual day of conception, the exact time and date of birth, or the exact time of death. These are divine secrets God holds as the original Creator, all for His purpose. All mankind can do is estimate, speculate, attempt to regenerate, but never duplicate God's fingerprint on humanity. All of this is unfathomable to our human minds, which proves there is something greater outside of our human existence, where His precepts reside. Only our Creator, the original scientist, whose words contained the biological nucleus that began and sustains all things, can explain and reveal to humanity what He wants us to know. Since He is outside of our world, our earthly scientists have made it their life's goal to unpack what was already finished in God's realm.

This is why their outcomes are called theories. They are just educated guesses, because the original biology did not come from within the earth but from beyond the earth. Honestly, the proof that we have scientists solidifies the fact that there is a God. God holds the patent to His precepts, and He will only reveal to man as He wills. The point is that we need to explore the scriptures to know what we can know and not elaborate on what we do not know. In the following chapter, I will show you examples of His precepts.

CHAPTER 3

PRECEPTS ARE FOUND THROUGH STUDY

I became intrigued to find out what and where the precepts were. One of the questions I have always had is "What happened before the earth came into existence?" In my personal relationship with God through the Holy Spirit, I asked Him the question, "Why didn't you start the Bible with your precepts?" To me, it would have made things a little clearer. However, in his infinite wisdom I realized He knew what He was doing and how dare I think for Him.

I don't want to oversimplify it, but seeking to understand this life God has created for Himself can be like playing "Where's Waldo." The "Where's Waldo" puzzle used to be found in a kids' magazine called *Highlights* years ago. It was a collage of hundreds of items in the center page of the magazine, and the goal was to

Precepts Are Found Through Study

find Waldo. His image was given to you so that you could look for him amid the crowded images. The children who started the search that did not give up would eventually find him, but the ones who did not want to invest that much time would give it a glance, make excuses, or move on to other puzzles that were easier to feel successful at.

The scriptures tell us that we did not seek God, but He revealed Himself to us (Isaiah 65:1 and John 15:16). So, it is now our turn to seek the one who found us. He provided the scriptures to us to become the official source to start our journey to know Him, to use and understand His words within their cultural context and definitions to get His pure meaning and translation. Let me say here, understanding God is not just an intellectual or mental exercise of the study of the Bible. We must obtain His knowledge (information), get understanding (comprehension) of it and then we will have to use wisdom to apply what we read. This all comes in conjunction with being in relationship with Him so that He can reveal to us the Spirit of His nature and character. Without knowing that, our interpretation will be inaccurate. For example, lawyers sometime use the term "the spirit of the law" as a part of their argument. Let me explain.

There is the "letter of the law," and there is the "spirit of the law." The letter of the law is composed of the actual words documented, for instance, *"Thou shalt have no other gods before me"* (Exodus 20:3). The spirit of that law has additional social and/or moral intentions that address gods as anything, i.e. our spouse, job, home, children, family etc.., before our relationship with God. It is not that He is against having relationship with

Precepts Are Found Through Study

our family, having a job, our children etc rather it should never be at the expense of making Him first in our lives.

What I found is that when we stop short in our investigation or seeking the truth, our conclusions will come up short of His truth. Jesus specifically told us to seek the kingdom of God and His righteousness and all the things we desire will be added (Matthew 6:33). He never said He put everything in the Bible chronologically for us; we assumed that. He left us clues about His realm, scriptures that support his laws, commands and principals, but they are hidden in plain sight where only the seeker would find those precious precepts that would bring more depth to our understanding of His world. The reason we overlook the clues is because of what I talked about earlier: we see and interpret things out of our limited experience and education would often rather be told what we need to know that do our own personal study.

Moreover, what I am about to show you is the result of a word study that helped me close the gap in my understanding of the timing of spiritual actions during God's creation process and how the timing of those events impacted my interpretation of the scriptures, i.e., His precepts. Here are some phrases from the scriptures that provide us with more revelation into His realm. I am only going to provide you an example of one of the below phrases that reveal His world before the earth was. You will be amazed, and I'm sure it will prompt you into further study. (See appendix I for more information.)

- before the foundation of the world
- from the foundation of the world
- before ordained

- ancient times
- afore prepared unto glory
- before the world began
- in the beginning
- from the beginning of creation

The first example is Ephesians 1:4, *"According as he hath chosen us in him before the foundation of the world, that we should be holy and without blame before him in love."*

I had read that scripture and quoted it many times, but the words *"before the foundation of the world"* had never jumped out at me. I just put this scripture into the predestination bucket and left it there. However, when taking those words into consideration, it made me ask the question of why God would influence the writer to use that phrase. From that question, several things became impressed upon my thoughts:

- First, humanity was on God's mind before He physically created the earth, i.e., man predates earth. That is kind of awesome to think about.
- Second, this positioned humanity in Jesus, being impregnated, as if it were predestined to have His DNA, which is why we can call Him Father.
- Third, it pre-solved how mankind could be redeemed by Jesus, because we were originally in His custody, with Him as our parent, our legal guardian. Whether we like it or not, all of humanity carries His DNA, which is our identifying marker. However, while we can physically reject and/or become emancipated from our parents by our own

will, we cannot change our spiritual heritage. His DNA is in the blood, and the blood is where life is, of which we all are from.

What I found is that, sprinkled throughout the scriptures—and not in chronological order—God uses words to give us insight to His realm, but if we don't inspect or dissect the words, we will miss their intended meaning. The scripture in 2 Timothy 2:15 says to *"study to show thyself approved unto God a workman that needeth not to be ashamed, rightly dividing the word of truth,"* and as I mentioned earlier, Matthew 6:33 says, *"Seek ye first the kingdom of God, and his righteousness; and all these things shall be added unto you."*

These scriptures were not addressed to leaders, but rather to everyone who desires to know Him. God has given us spiritual and natural tools to find Him. Whether through worship, prayer, reading His words, or revelation from The Spirit speaking to us, He will supply us with what we need and what we need to know. Don't just rely upon the many online speakers, study aids, educational degrees, and reference materials that bring light and illumination to our understanding; He must be a part of the equation. That is what the Holy Spirit is here for, to guide us into all truth, which is one truth, not many. Take the time to study out the other phrases I outlined above and see how He will reveal Himself to you so you can add to your arsenal of truths about His word.

Here's another example of using this way of study to explore questions you still may have about the scriptures. Something I always struggled with is how God could and would conceive the idea concerning something with diabolical character in His world, that being Satan. So, in closing this chapter, we must talk about the precepts of Satan's rebellion. I will show you scriptures that speak to his beginning and his end.

When we read the Bible linearly, Satan abruptly shows up just after creation with no storyline, no history as the serpent. We don't know how he got there, who put him there, what his objective was, or why he was referenced as an earthly animal. That being said, we filled in the blanks from our own mind and created our own narrative. Some have surmised that since the Bible says God created all things, and the serpent is an evil thing, God created evil. This is great deductive reasoning, but God is not evil, nor did He create evil. His precept of free will is the catalyst of evil, in that free will makes evil possible. Truthfully, granting man free will was the greatest act of love He could give mankind. In His wisdom, God knew that opening the capability for man to choose could lead to outcomes He never desired. From a human standpoint, we would say God took a big risk in making this decision, but from His perspective, He knew the product He designed and desired for man, and He pre-solved every possibility before it occurred.

All things created in God's realm have a divine purpose for His world. Those purposes were never meant to become distorted, but free will opened the door to make evil possible. As a good Father, He provided a path with boundaries and guardrails, believing that man would freely choose His plans over himself. We must remember that free will is not free if choice is taken away. If we had no free will, we would be robots, which is the form of what man is creating today with artificial intelligence. Free will is the embodiment of the real love God has for His creation despite His knowing its potential misuse.

So, where did this serpent come from? Initially, when I was taught the Bible, I did not question what I was told, I just believed the story, even if detailed explanations were left out. As I got older, my curiosity wanted answers. All throughout my personal and academic studies in seminary, I still did not find the answer to those questions, and at the same time, it did not hinder my belief in God. I planted my feet, moved forward by faith with what I knew and believed, and kept it moving.

About seven years ago, I stumbled upon a teaching from Dr. Paula A. Price about Satan's origin that I had never heard. What I experienced in that teaching was like stumbling across a shade tree and a breeze in the middle of a hot desert. So, Her book, Before the Garden, provoked me to study more. In my study God brought three passages of scripture to my mind that spoke of Satan's origin that I had never put together. In this process, I found that it was not the lack of teaching from former leaders that left me without answer rather, I had a responsibility to commit to my own study to develop my personal spiritual growth. I had religiously looked to my church leaders to serve me with what I needed to be spiritually healthy, hoping that would sustain me. However, there comes a point of maturity where it was time for me to follow the prompting of the Spirit to act by studying for myself. If we are honest with ourselves, most of our spiritual understanding is made up of what we have heard and not what we have studied. I know I am painting a broad brush, so if that is not your story, don't be offended. If it is your story, we still have an opportunity to get His knowledge, understanding, and wisdom.

Satan's rise and fall

The scriptures that present us with Satan's beginnings, character, motivation, and plight are as follows. Ezekiel 28:13-19 speaks of the original nature of Lucifer, later to be called Satan. He was an angel within the inner sanctum of heaven next to God and his pride became his demise. Isaiah 14:12-17 speaks of Satan being cast out of heaven for his rebellion of desiring to be like God. Revelation 12:4 speaks to a war in heaven where Satan fought with God's angels and was cast to the earth while taking one third of heavens angels with him. Luke 10:18 is where Jesus told his disciples that he saw Satan fall like lightning from heaven. Lastly, Genesis 1:2 defines the condition of the components of the atmosphere when the earth was made.

What I am proposing here is that all of the events mentioned took place in heaven and not on earth. There is an operation of heaven, consisting of God and the divine creatures He created, the makeup of his staff and structure. They are called angels with varying roles, e.g., warrior angels like Michael, messenger angels like Gabriel, seraphim who are part human in form, cherubim, and other celestial beings. Lucifer was one of those angels who held a position. His name means "light bearer." He obviously had position and access to God to see and hear some of the inner conversations concerning God's plan for the earth and humanity. Somewhere in that process, pride rose up, and he plotted to unseat God. The operation of heaven must have been very awesome for Lucifer to conceive a coup attempt against the government of God. This became proof to me that there were things going on in heaven besides the Godhead sitting in the throne room with

Precepts Are Found Through Study

His host of angels sitting around him crying "Holy, Holy, Holy" day and night.

I found yet another precept in Revelation 12, where Satan made his initial coup attempt on God taking one third of the angels with him, led me to question the chronology of events I was initially taught. I found it intriguing that the references in Revelation 12 had implications of a pre-earth existence. How was this happening at the end of the book? I was perplexed relating this to a pre-earth event. It was studying the Hebrew words in Genesis 1:2 that brought out imagery that speaks to the pre-earth atmospheric conditions when God spoke the earth into existence. In that verse, the writer used terminology that was very descriptive and distinct. He used words like "void," "without form," "dark," and a "deep watery abyss." The implication is that there was something previously in the spirit realm that was in earth atmosphere. As I broke down the bolded words based on their Hebrew definitions, I saw something with much greater implications. Below, I have taken the actual scripture from Genesis 1:2 and put the biblical definition in italicized within the parenthesis so that you can read it in it's full context.

> The **earth** (*land, country, ground*) was without **form** (*formlessness, confusion, unreality, place of chaos*), and **void** (*empty*); and **darkness** (*misery, destruction, death, ignorance, sorrow, wickedness*) was **on the face** (*in the presence of*) of the **deep** (*abyss—as a surging mass of water*). And the **Spirit** (*Wind/Breath*) of God was **hovering** (*brooding—thinking deeply about something that makes one unhappy*) **over the face** (*in the presence*) of the **waters** (*urine, semen, piss*).

Precepts Are Found Through Study

Wow, this is a gamechanger from how someone would read it from their own culture and language. That earth appears to have all the aspects that represent Satan after being cast to the earth. In heaven his name and character represented light, and now he is darkness. In heaven he was in peace, and after his expulsion he is now chaos. He went from the presence of God and is now a part of the watery existence of feces. And then in Genesis 1:3, God said, "Let there be light." Light on what? Light to dispel the darkness which was existent in the stratosphere. The darkness was not just the absence of light; the darkness is now Satan embodied.

I did not make up these definitions; therefore, the scriptures reveal that God created the earth within this atmospheric confusion where Satan was cast, which enabled him to be a spirit in the earth realm when God finished. So then I asked God, "If Satan was within the spiritual realm of the earth, then how can you call what you created good?" His reply to me was, "It is good because Satan was never a threat to my plan. Everything I created revolved around my purpose, not his." My next question to God was, "Why could you not just have annihilated him after his rebellion, seeing that within three chapters in the book, he caused a division between you and mankind?" God answered, "No, I could not annihilate him, because everything I create is eternal." He further spoke to me, stating, "I pre-solved all of this prior to the earth's creation.

There are two places of eternity, one being heaven and the other hell. In my original plan, heaven was for those who acknowledge Jesus as Lord and live for Him, and hell was for the devil and those who reject Jesus as stated in Matthew 25:41." All of His plans are eternal, and He committed to them from the beginning regardless of our choices. He upholds His world by His words.

Now, this is where the remaining scriptures in Revelation 12 and Luke 10 come into play. If Revelation 12:9 is an eschatological event that propelled Satan out of heaven for the last time, then how do we explain the atmospheric conditions of the stratosphere of heaven when God created the earth in Genesis chapter 1? Secondly, why would Jesus make a pre-earth statement to the 70 disciples after they were sent out that He saw Satan fall from heaven? If Satan's fall from heaven was a future event as thought of in Revelation 12:10, then Satan must have fallen from heaven multiple times, right?

We can see that Jesus was further confirming to His disciples who He was by what He had witnessed. As I said earlier, the events of scripture are not necessarily written in chronological order, and only through careful seeking and revelation can the sequence of these events be understood. You don't have to take my word for it, study and seek revelation, just don't hold on to the truth that you have only heard and not studied for yourself. Lastly, it is my hope that these scripture references fill in any major gaps in your understanding as they did mine, which assured me that God never changed His mind or altered His plans for humanity.

Spiritual Stockholm Syndrome: How the light dims

With Satan's fall to earth, this opened more questions for me. So, I asked God how it could be that man is unaware of our captivity under Satan's rule, and He likened it to a worldly concept humanity has termed Stockholm Syndrome. Stockholm Syndrome is a psychological condition where a victim identifies and empathizes with their captor so much that they don't attempt to leave them.[3] The psychological response shows up when the captive begins to identify closely with his or her captors, as well as with their agenda and demands. The syndrome is marked not only by a positive bond between captive and captor but also by a negative attitude on behalf of the captive toward authorities who threaten the captor-captive relationship.[4] This is the spiritual impact Satan has on mankind.

First, let me give you a natural analogy of this syndrome. It can be likened to how we as humans adjust to physical darkness with our eyes. For example, on any given day as the sun starts to go down, the light silently creeps out of a room, and the day transitions into the evening, it happens very subtly, almost undetectably, because we have an innate response in our bodies that tells our eyes to adjust to the light. For example, if you have been sitting in a room doing homework or working in the daylight, and the light gets dimmer as the day goes on, someone might come in and say, "Why is it so dark in here? How can you see?"

Our typical response is that we can see fine, and we tell the person that they are the one who needs all that light. Is the person who is sitting in the dark right, or have they just adjusted to the darkness so much that the brightness of the light has lost its significance and value to them? When we sit in dim lighting, we can be functional, but what we don't know is that we are putting unnecessary strain on our eyes, which in turn makes it harder for us to focus and creates negative impacts on our brains.

Precepts Are Found Through Study

The same holds true for the grip of darkness that Satan has on our lives before we come to acknowledge Jesus, the light of the world. We must know that we all started our journey of life in this darkness because of Adam's sin. Romans 5:12 says, *"Wherefore, as by one man sin entered into the world, and death by sin; and so death passed upon all men, for that all have sinned."* That being said, no man comes into this world knowing the true light. We are all living in darkness until we opt out by responding to the call from Jesus to follow Him. Only Adam was aware of the true light before his fall and the immediate impact of that darkness that came upon them in the garden (Genesis 3:7-13). This is where his new nature showed up: lying, blame shifting, hiding, and not taking full responsibility for his actions.

So here we are today, exhibiting that same nature and character, not realizing that we inherited it as the offspring of the first Adam. We have this false sense of security that we are in the brightest light, and when anyone says something to the contrary, our pride rises up and we stamp out the opportunity for the great light to be seen. As I said earlier, dim light does not make one unproductive, ineffective, or inoperable; rather, we adjust to it as a normal part of our life, never knowing that how we are existing is abnormal for a creature of God. The longer we resist the acceptance of Jesus in our lives, the longer the grip of darkness will continue to shroud our mind, resulting in blindness to the true light of Jesus. This is where we fall under the Spiritual Stockholm Syndrome effect, blind to the fact that we have been detained by and fallen in love with our captor, Satan, the prince of darkness. We have succumbed to his nature and character, which Timothy references in 2 Timothy 3:2-4 (NRSV):

Precepts Are Found Through Study

> *For people will be lovers of themselves, lovers of money, boasters, arrogant, abusive, disobedient to their parents, ungrateful, unholy, inhuman, implacable, slanderers, profligates, brutes, haters of good, treacherous, reckless, swollen with conceit, lovers of pleasure rather than lovers of God.*

Furthermore, when we are in darkness, we can't see that we are estranged from God. This is why scripture identifies one of the names of Jesus as the Light of the World (John 8:12). At the time of the start of Jesus' ministry, Matthew spoke of the prophecy of Isaiah which confirms this, as it says, *"The people which sat in darkness saw a great light, and to them which sat in the region and shadow of death, light is sprung up"* (Matthew 4:16). Jesus would be the pathway for man's redemption to be loosed from the grips of Satan and to be changed and transformed by the light of Christ. Another confirming scripture is found in 2 Timothy 2:26, which states, *"And that they may recover themselves out of the snare of the devil, who are taken captive by him at his will."* Lastly, Colossians 1:13 describes God: *"Who hath delivered us from the power of darkness, and hath translated us into the kingdom of his dear Son."* It is hard for man to comprehend that he is not in control of himself. Our pride must be broken, and we must relent of the truth that we are being influenced by another source, another voice that has been with us since birth.

Have you ever thought about the fact that at times when you did something of your own free will, you asked yourself afterward, "Why did I do that?" The real question is, who orchestrated the thought that put you in this situation, knowing that you already had a forethought that you should not do it? How do you account for that duality? If our thoughts are our own thoughts, then how does an opposing thought enter our minds? Think on this for a moment. Who is instructing man from outside of himself if there are no other spiritual authorities contending for his mind? Where do you think the thoughts come from? If we listen to ourselves, we must know that outside of a renewed mind in Christ, we are caving into the ideas from Satan. I do not personally subscribe to the thinking that man fights against his own personal thoughts. We are either influenced by the old man/nature in us (Satan) or the renewed man/nature of Christ. (See appendix II for more scriptural references.) Man is not okay without God.

Let's turn our eyes to the spiritual reality of this syndrome. When God created man with His hands from the dust, man was nothing more than a dirt body. However, when He breathed His breath, His life force, His Spirit into man, he became a living soul. God's breath was not just wind or air, but rather the creative force from His mouth which He used to speak the universe into existence, all of which brought forth life. However, with man, God put His identifying markers, His DNA—His intellect, His mind, His thoughts, His desires—and at the same time gave man free will. Man was full of God, and they were one. He did not have to teach man evil or advise him regarding the subject, as it was unnecessary. Adam saw God as his only source, as no antagonist had corrupted their communication. Adam experienced God's love, affection, admiration, protection, covering, and constant communion. Essentially, man had no desire to use his free will, or even needed to be cognizant of it, as God was everything to him. It was the sovereignty of God to give man free will because He knew one day man's loyalty would be challenged, and God set it up to prove the authentic relationship by man's submission and not by force. Before we judge this perspective or any other premise of God, we must remember that God was crafting His world, with His creation, for His purpose and His plan, not what humans have surmised it to be. So, the inflection point would be to see if man would maintain his oneness with God, or if he would exercise his free will to entertain another voice.

I then asked God, "But how would man exercise his free will when there was no one else on the planet but the four of you in the beginning?" God said, "Who told you that only humans spoke on the earth? All life is my creation. It bears my name, it carries out my purpose, it knows my voice. Because of this, all things co-exist and work in synergy with man utilizing his delegated authority to have dominion, to subdue the earth." Do you recall the scripture in Romans 8:19 that says that all of creation is waiting for the manifestation of the sons of God? This implies that creation has eyes. Deuteronomy 20:8, when God told Moses to speak to the rock in front of the people so it would give water, implies that creation has ears.

In Luke 19:40, Jesus tells the Pharisees that He will not shut up His disciples because if He did, the stones would cry out—this implies that creation can speak. Lastly, Deuteronomy 30:19, where God says He will call heaven and earth as a witness against us, implies that all of creation is at His behest. "Furthermore," God reminded me again, "this is my world, and it does not fit the confines of your human mind of what is possible and not possible." We must remember this because we easily defer to our finite knowledge, which cannot contend with our Creator.

Having said this, God continued, "When I cast Satan to the earth due to his rebellion, he became an illegal spirit with no power or authority because I stripped him of all his heavenly qualities. He remained a spirit. Nevertheless, Satan's mission was still the same, to have power over all creation. Having been in my presence in his former estate, he knew my operation and stance on loyalty. His mastermind conceived how he could still get back at me through my creation. So he devised a plan to enter the earth. The only way he could become legal in the earth was to gain illegal access by way of an earthly creation. That he did, as he too beguiled the serpent to use his body to speak to Adam female. The rest is history, as once he tricked her to listen to him, she got Adam to agree—they did follow his suggestion, and they unknowingly gave him rulership over their lives."

How do we know this? Because the serpent was cursed for his actions just as the man and woman were. Their disobedience opened their lives up to another kingdom that they were unaware of. The kingdom of darkness had veiled their eyes so much, so they attempted to cover themselves. Evil had now come upon them. Everything about them changed: their eyesight, emotions, demeanour, and character. I believe that at that instance, the Holy Spirit left their presence. Satan was celebrating because he believed he has the whole world at his behest, with man castrated from God just as he was. He now held the power and control of the destiny of man—except for the fact that God had already pre-solved how he would legally get man back, which will be discussed in later chapters.

Now that man had been taken captive under this new authority, God was no longer his guide or confident. The kingdom of darkness was now lording over man and the earth. It became very apparent that darkness and the depravity of man was moving ahead full steam. The impact of Satan's second coup was in full effect, as we see the first murder occurring in the first family immediately after the fall. Satan's spiritual authority, his Stockholm Syndrome effect, over mankind's soul offers a clear picture of why Adam never fought back against his captor. I find it interesting that at no point in scripture do we see Adam or Eve lamenting about their former life or desire to get back to God. As time went on, more and more sinister behaviours were occurring in the earth. We are told in Genesis 6:5-6, *"And God saw the wickedness of man was great in the earth, and that every imagination of the thoughts of his heart was only evil continually. And it repented the Lord that he had made man on the earth, and it grieved him at his heart."*

The sovereignty of God

The effects of Adam's treason continued to grow and grow until God said "enough" and brought the flood to destroy the earth, except for eight people and the representatives of the animal kingdom that He would use to begin the earth again. This action was not a display of God changing His mind about His original creation, but rather demonstrating that His world will not be upended by any force. He stayed committed to His plan. Up to this point, mankind had never experienced such an event as this. If God had never shown Himself with this level of authority over all creation, we would never believe His promises of how He would move heaven and earth on our behalf, or how He would bring His plan to completion at the end of the age by destroying this earth and creating a new heaven and earth.

Sovereignty is not a concept that we utilize in the United States, as we live in a democratic system that never allows anyone to have that much control over us—or so we think. When we try to apply our human minds to how and why God moves the way He does, we are quietly saying that we know more than He does. But how can we, the creation, advise the Creator on His actions? As the scripture says in Isaiah 55:8-9,

> *For my thoughts are not your thoughts, neither are your ways my ways, saith the Lord. For as the heavens are higher than the earth, so are my ways higher than your ways, and my thoughts than your thoughts.*

The authority of the Creator

Does this make God egocentric, a control freak, bipolar, or a narcissist? No—as the authority or the creator, one has the right to establish the purpose, use, and definition of their creation. Think of it like how a manufacturer treats its product. They create a product, the consumer purchases it, and they provide the consumer with an owner's instruction manual. Within that manual, the manufacturer outlines what the product is capable of, its maintenance schedule, its parts, its guarantees, warranties, and certifications. It clearly defines how to handle any situation that may arise due to malfunction, distortion, misuse, or abuse of the product. It provides instructions on what to do if a malfunction occurs. Lastly, if the item has to be returned, they will have the right to pass judgment on what the cause was and to either make it good by sending the consumer a new product or to advise them of the misuse of the product. Often when we misuse a product, we want to push the limits of the manufacturer in hopes they will not notice our mishap. This is what sovereignty is: the creator having authority over what he created.

God shows us proof of His authority

When we look at most of the sovereign acts of God, our human minds want to ask, "Why did those actions have to be handled in that manner? Wasn't there a better way?" We think of acts like allowing Satan to be in the earth, Cain to kill Abel, the people of Babel to attempt to build a tower to heaven, the earth to be flooded. Sending destruction to Sodom and Gomorrah, allowing innocent children to die and mothers to mourn so that Moses' and Jesus' lives could be spared, allowing Satan to try Job, and Joseph to be put in a pit by his brothers. The opening of the Red Sea, the walls of Jericho falling, His command for the destruction of life of those who were not a part of His covenant, the swallowing of his own prophet by a big fish for three days. Allowing His servants Shadrach, Meshach, and Abednego to go into the fiery furnace, and Daniel to be put into the lion's den. These are just a microcosm of the sovereign acts that He allowed and/or orchestrated after man rejected Him in the garden. As I said earlier, God will use any imperfection, mistake, mishap, or even our wilful sin to complete His purpose to provide man with ultimate proof of His authority, power, and loyalty to what He says.

These acts are not just isolated incidents for us to memorize and internalize for our knowledge; rather, they offer us insight into the Father's eternal plans, which often conflict with our human sentiments. Some of His sovereign acts will not make sense in the time they are committed but will provide a launching point as you study scripture, and this will allow you to make connections about the consistency of His character. For example, we ask, "Did He need to flood the earth? What was his point? That was such a harsh thing, to kill all those people." But what if He chose that sovereign act because He wanted humanity to know the full capability of His power and authority as a reference point; that He is ruler over all things in heaven and earth.

We don't like to stop and consider what had to die so that God's plan could live. We often allow those acts to present a dilemma or a bittersweet victory, or we may even see them as evil, arrogant, and non-loving actions. The result is a distortion of our understanding of Him, which opens the door for our emotions to take on a mentality that becomes for or against God based on our reality. Humans are a complex people, because when God's sovereign acts call for Him to step in and grant us victory, we take the win, but when a situation occurs that appears to have devastating consequences to an individual or group, we question His action or inaction. If we are not careful, we take sides, allowing our sentiments to prevail over His purposes. Our flesh always wants to find another way for everyone to win and no one to lose. Again, we have to remember that this is His world.

The lesson of submission

What we must learn is that the submission process requires us to follow and trust Him. Submission is not about our agreement, but rather about our willingness to trust Him by laying down our own agenda and coming completely under His mission, even when it hurts. It is not situational. Submitting to God does not mean He does not care about our feelings. His goal is to show us that only through submission will we know the true freedom we have in the earth.

Man's responsibility is to pivot from the mindset of what we think God's role should be and to come under His wings, where He will nurture us and restore us from the effects of Stockholm Syndrome. He will bring us back to His original design to look, act, give, and love like Him, bearing His nature and character. This is summed up in John 17:3 when Jesus said, *"And this is life eternal, that they might know thee the only true God, and Jesus Christ whom thou has sent."* This solidifies why we can have hope and trust in God as the master estate planner, the one who thoroughly planned and invested in the future of all creation. Life with God is not about our spouses, children, brothers or sisters, etc. It is about our life with Him now and in eternity, never forgetting we were born for Him. To literally fill His world as this life on this planet is not about our own thoughts, plans, opinions, morals, speculations, reasons, rationalizations, or ideas. This is His world crafted for His purpose and His plan.

Part II:

His Purpose – Jesus

CHAPTER 4

UNDERSTANDING GOD'S PURPOSE

Purpose has to do with answering the question of "Why?" When we don't understand the "why" of things, we make assumptions by filling in the gaps based on our own feelings, experiences, and even our ignorance. Because we find our theory plausible, we become the voice of truth to ourselves, and if we get enough support from others who will buy into our conclusions, we feel credible. When it comes to God's original intention, do we really understand Him? If we don't, then we are unconsciously spreading error. Who better to give understanding than the Creator who authored and inspired His selected individuals to provide written proof of His truth? As a side note, don't get distracted by the writers of the Bible, as they are not on trial; it is the word of God that is on trial. Our focus is to be upon Him. Only the enemy wants to cloud God's truth with the imagery, the authors' naming conventions, the artistic impressions of Jesus, etc. He tells us in Proverbs 4:7, *"With all thy getting get understanding."* I have never been one to just take things at face value. The desire to know the real truth is embedded in my makeup, and I believe that is the truth for all mankind.

People often choose to feel a certain kind of way when I bring more truth on a subject than they have taken the time to study. I do this not to put myself above them, but rather to show that there is always more to know. We must dig deeper to get to the truth as the Holy Spirit reveals. Diamonds are not found on the surface, they must be excavated and extracted, and that takes work. Finding truth is not for the faint at heart. It takes commitment and dedication and relationship with the Holy Spirit. So, let's explore the "why" or purpose in this section.

Appreciating God's purpose

But first, how can we appreciate God's world if we don't really understand His purpose for all of His creation? Wouldn't it serve us better to read through His words through His lenses, ensuring we are not adjusting His purpose based on what we know and have seen and experienced in our world? Have you ever set out with a plan to do or create something, and somewhere in the process, people misinterpreted your intentions and/or use of your creation? By the behaviours exhibited, you would know who understood or misunderstood the intentions of your plan or creation. It is easy to fall in this trap of letting others define things for us. I am not saying that the ministers of the gospel are not needed. What I am saying is that everyone has a responsibility to know the scriptures for themselves. If we don't, then how do we know the leader is following the scriptures? What about Jim Jones, David Koresh, Charles Manson, Heaven's Gate, and other cults? They enticed many people to their death because of their ignorance of God's word. Scripture says God set leaders in the church (Ephesians 4:11-12), and it also tells us to study to show ourselves approved (2 Timothy 2:15).

Another example concerning the importance of study is knowing the natural laws of our society. Without knowing the intent of the law, we may read or know parts of it but find ourselves ignorant and suffer the consequences. In other words, if we superimpose our fallen nature to guide our understanding, it will lead to error. We do this in the natural when we see and exceed the established speed limit signs and get mad when we are ticketed by the police for breaking the law. The signs and laws are posted to protect us. However, when we convince ourselves that we have justification for our disobedience, we look for leniency, but the officer still gives us a ticket. If the officer gives you leniency, that works out great for you, but their decision does not change the law. Our reasoning and justifications are not sufficient to supersede natural or spiritual laws, as there will be consequences. This makes understanding Jesus paramount.

In this chapter, I am not going into the details of Jesus' birth, death, or resurrection on the earth; rather, I am more focused on His purpose for being in the earth. I write these things not to presume anyone reading this book is ignorant, but to expand our spiritual capacity to ensure we have not stopped ingesting spiritual food because we are satisfied with what has been presented to us. I would presume that many of us do not eat many five course meals, if any at all, because who has time to do that? However, when that kind of meal is presented, you must be patient and wait for each serving, as they will complement each other and be fulfilling at the end.

At this point, I'm sure most believers are thinking, "I know why Jesus came," but let me give you all the courses of His life so you can be sure you haven't missed anything. For example, if we read the Bible linearly, we could walk away thinking that Jesus was not in the Old Testament but became evident only at His birth to the virgin Mary. He actually was spiritually commissioned by God in Genesis 3:15 when He said, *"And I will put enmity between thee and the woman, and between thy seed and her seed; it shall bruise thy head, and thou shalt bruise his heel."* Notice here that God does not mention Jesus specifically by name, so if you are reading the Bible based on the letter, you will misapply Jesus' entrance and purpose. The nature of God is displayed in His use of people, places, and names to lead man down a path to connect the dots and get to His true meaning. I don't understand why God did it this way, but through reading the scriptures, it's all hidden in plain sight. We must seek. Here is a perfect example of Him giving us glimpses into Jesus' past very subtly, hidden away in Proverbs 8:23-30, which says,

> *I was set up from everlasting, from the beginning, or ever the earth was. When there were no depths, I was brought forth; when there were no fountains abounding with water. Before the mountains were settled, before the hills was I brought forth: While as yet he had not made the earth, nor the fields, nor the highest part of the dust of the world. When he prepared the heavens, I was there: when he set a compass upon the face of the depth: When*

> *he established the clouds above: when he strengthened the fountains of the deep: When he gave to the sea his decree, that the waters should not pass his commandment: when he appointed the foundations of the earth: Then I was by him, as one brought up with him: and I was daily his delight, rejoicing always before him.*

Through looking up the Hebrew definition of the phrase *"set up from everlasting"* in verse 23, I found that the word translated as "everlasting" is defined in Hebrew as perpetual, continuous existence. This was a revelation to me, as I was basing my interpretation on the literal reading of the scriptures and thought that if Jesus' name was not written in the Old Testament, He did not exist yet. As I read the scriptures, I was following the trail that the Savior, the Messiah, the soon coming King was yet to arrive. I was right physically but not spiritually. My mind was affixed on "my truth" that He was not born yet. Finding this scripture made me revisit my truth, and then other scriptures came to light, namely Genesis 1:26, where God said, *"Let us make man in our image, after our likeness."* My question then became, "Who was the 'us'?" Again, in "my truth," if the name of Jesus or the Holy Spirit was not written with those exact words, then they did not exist yet. I was moving in my chronological, finite understanding of time, not knowing that God had already gone before me in His eternal time.

He knows the end from the beginning

Because God has already gone before us, scripture tells us that He already knows whose names are written in the Lamb's book of life, as well as the fact that Jesus was slain before the foundation of the world. How could these things have been written if the end of the world has still not come? Therein lies the question and the answer. In God's eternal realm, these things have already been done. Man is currently walking into the future that is God's past. Therefore, God's past is man's future. Again, these scriptures baffled my mind, and it required me to rethink my understanding to accept that He already knows the outcome of His plan because He walked it out before He created anything. My truth had to change, as He is not in time—He is eternal, outside of time, and we are on His eternal continuum. This means that we have always spiritually lived in Christ (Ephesians 1:4) and we will never spiritually die because we are eternal. Chronological time is a blip on God's eternal continuum. When Adam rebelled, it turned on a physical death clock for our time upon the earth as well as a death of our spiritual connection with God. With sin and separation from God now sown in the earth, God had to invoke His perpetual plan to redeem man from this contaminated state. Death, hell, and the grave must be reconciled so that God's eternal continuum will not be disrupted.

This was all planned prior to our existence. How do we know this? Because God is not constantly altering and adjusting to man's ups and downs or twist and turns. He could not be subjected to His creation's whims, as then He would be a caterer and not the creator of man. Furthermore, the prophecies that were recorded are also accurate, because He completed everything before it started. I'm saying all of this to say that if we place God in our chronological time dimension, we will err in our understanding of things that have happened and will happen in our lives.

Understanding God's Purpose

To further explain the importance of this, let me share how common statements spoken from pulpits formulate our misunderstanding of how eternity and time should be addressed. The first one is "God knows what you are going to do before you do it," and the second is "God is all knowing." Those statements are truly stated, but they must be put into the proper context of His eternal continuum.

Growing up in church in my teens and early twenties, upon hearing those statements, I would say to myself, "If God is walking with me in time, why would He not stop me, or why would He allow these negative things to happen to me? Does He not like me?" Moreover, when I sat in services and heard the preacher say that God is all knowing, it made me cringe, as I knew of people who had been molested by family members or raped by strangers, and I would think, "I wonder what those people would think if they were sitting in this service. If I were them, I would say, 'God, if you knew it, why didn't you stop it?'" Then the icing on the cake statement I would hear from the pulpit is that "you had to go through that for God to get the glory." I would say to myself, "What glory? People are still traumatized by the past—it was hurtful, frightening, damaging to their emotions." I thought, "Why would He allow people to be victimized over the course of their lives, knowing it was happening?"

So my summation was, "If these statements are true, then what good does it do God to know everything and not stop it?" It just did not seem to be fair. How could I trust someone who knows what will happen and yet not stop it? All this time I thought He was sanctioning my and others' trauma. This was also confirmed by leaders in the church and other church members who would say, "Child, it was God's plan."

What I found out was that those events were not Him sanctioning the activity in that moment it occurred, as that was my present and His past. He already knew from eternity what depravity was in man, because of sin and its potential to produce evil. Nevertheless, God pre-solved, not prevented, its effects through Jesus. I know you still have some real questions as to why these things were allowed to happen. The best explanation He revealed to me was that He is in control of everything, but He does not control everybody due to free will, as man is subject to the master he chooses to bow to. But God, through Jesus, took on all sin, in spite of the evil committed against us or the sin we committed against ourselves, to provide us with the ability to overcome all evil. Jesus provided a pathway for us to conquer and overcome all tests, trials, or evil that would befall us. Jesus does not remove it, He takes us through it by our faith.

In order to see the thread of God's plan, we had to trace Jesus' history back to the beginning, knowing that the world God was creating was not coincidental or happenstance. He was intentional about every aspect of the outcomes He desired. As the Alpha and Omega, He had eternal foresight and hindsight to make plans despite his future creation's action or inaction. All of God's arsenal was prepared for every possible outcome. So when it appeared that Satan had fractured heaven with his revolt and later kidnapping of humanity on earth, God's contingency plan was already prepared to recover. Jesus was not an afterthought. As we confirmed earlier, He was with God in the beginning to take on the role of the Savior if man used his free will to rebel against the Father. God's purpose for Jesus never changed. Let's dive further into where Jesus fits within the blueprint God was constructing.

God's blueprint

Blueprints are a fundamental part of an architect's or engineer's job to create plans for building a sound structure. They establish the height, width, doors, windows, and walls that ensure that the integrity of what is being built will be able to withstand its planned functionality and usability. Basically, they confirm that the building will be fit for what is going to be accomplished in it. God has a blueprint, as the architect of His kingdom, His original design from the beginning, was to extend His heavenly kingdom to earth and give man dominion over it. He pre-solved the entire construct of His blueprint from the beginning.

To carry out His mandate, He needed a population of people to represent Him as stated in Matthew 6:10: *"...thy kingdom come, thy will be done on earth as it is in heaven."* His extension plan required people. His plan created male and female and equipped them with the means to reproduce His offspring that came from His prototype, Adam. The world He was producing was never about man's personal wants or desires; rather, it was for man to carry out His desires. All God had to do was to create one prototype (Adam) from which all humanity would reproduce after. Yes, Adam female was taken out of Adam and therefore shared the design qualities, but not the same specifications by design. Through them, He would facilitate getting His creation into His planet.

As far as we know, God never advised man how to procreate; it was built into the fiber of their being. Their desire for one another was innate, and their bodies were prepared with His creative intentions to produce offspring without their foreknowledge. He did not leave the reproductive decision for man or woman to decide, it was built in so He could get His world to come into being, just like with the animals. We can presume that he had no discussion with them about "if" they wanted children—it was built in. Man was set up to desire and engage in the process of sexual intercourse, but he was never intended to control the outcome of it.

Moreover, to substantiate this thought, He gave females at birth over 1-2 million eggs, and at puberty they have somewhere around 300,000 eggs remaining for the rest of their life.[5] For the males at their maturity, they would release over 1 million sperm every time they participated in the procreation act, with no diminishing of their virility as they aged.[6] God made it so that it would only take one sperm out of the millions to penetrate the egg of a woman and create a human child. Think about it: neither man nor woman knows exactly when conception occurs, the gender of the child, or when its actual birth or death will occur. Science can only give us approximations. All men and women are responsible for is to commit the act. The only thing man could potentially control is to devise forms of contraception to stop it, or ways to abort.

It was never God's plan for us to interfere with His procreative process in any way. He did not need us to tamper with anything He had made. Having said this, it is evident that man was never to own the process of creating or ending life. This is why the lives of children are so important to God, He has an agenda for His creation and His planet (see appendix III for more information.) Psalm 116:15 says, *"The heaven, even the heavens, are the Lord's; but the earth he hath given to the children of men."* Just a side note, notice this verse does not say "to artificial intelligent beings" but "to the children of men." All His created forms of life belong to Him for His purpose; anything else is a counterfeit. It is only the effects of sin that have humanity now thinking that they have control over their bodies to produce life, end life, or create another form of life.

Adam was born with a blank slate, a consciousness that was not fully aware of. He did not know he was the prototype for all mankind, and he did not know the full extent of the meaning of death. He had never dealt with consequences or even had a need to consider them. As he freely developed in his life with God, He only knew to follow and obey his Creator. One thing to note is that God made no verbal covenant with Adam; he just existed with Him. Through that existence, Adam inherited the mind and Spirit of God, which is how he could name the animals. The only difference between Adam and God was that God is the sovereign ruler and Adam was His creation. God had to test man's free will, and He gave him one job: not to eat from the tree in the midst of the garden. Adam and the woman knew no adversary, but I surmise that the deception of the devil, after he hijacked the body of the serpent, was so alluring that instead of taking authority over the snake, they decided to listen to his conversation.

Note, I believe it is safe to say that man and animals could communicate with each other then, and it still works like that today.

Our pets understand us, and we understand them. Nevertheless, not knowing the full extent or gravity of the consequences they would face, Adam and the woman entertained the serpent's conversation, putting aside their dominion authority and utilizing their free will to go against the instruction given. That test did not destroy God's plan for man, as Jesus was on standby to crush the head of the serpent as spoken in Genesis 3:15.

Now we have experienced Adam, the original prototype and the blueprint for God's extension plan. We now see the impacts of free will on Adam and the depravity of man continually after the fall. With God's blueprint still in force, He redirected His plans through one family. After sin, what God did not get established through Adam by pure relationship He later established through a physical and spiritual covenant with Noah. He shut up Noah and his family along with a subsection of the animal kingdom in the Ark for their preservation to fulfil His plan. I know it is hard to swallow God killing off His own creation, but the intent of the Bible is to reveal His purpose. He continued revealing Himself through His chosen people's bloodline with Abraham, Noah's great-grandson, and his descendants. God created a chosen nation that He would call His children. This people would be the examples of the invisible God and His kingdom on earth via a blood covenant.

That covenant demonstrated His promise to Abraham, that through him all the families of the earth would be blessed. This blessing was the start of the promises that were to come to those who remained under the spiritual blueprint God had originally designed for Adam. What we find in the Old Testament is God constructing an external spiritual confidence in man that would eventually become an internal habitation, showing Himself as the access point of entry through a covenant relationship.

To prepare His chosen people to understand His blueprint, He worked with His designated earthly leaders to set up a governing structure to be followed that included leadership roles, laws, and a sacrificial system. This structure was more about who He is than a religious system. He was revealing Himself through types and shadows of the activities they had to go through. It's becoming clearer to me that God has established a pattern with His children where He never discloses all the insights of what He is doing and why. His goal is to see if we follow and trust Him, walking by faith and not by sight. The carrying out of these laws and rituals was not to conjure up, pacify, or placate Him; rather, it was a demonstration of their commitment and reverence to Him as their God in following His commands. He was showing them how commitment requires sacrifice, just as we know it today as faith. This is God forging the path of His purpose for mankind to commit their ways to Him as He continually does with us.

Man's desires

God has a blueprint, but our free will provides us a means to redirect His intentions; here are two examples in which man did just that. God gave them the Ten Commandments, and the rabbis responded with the mitzvot; God gave them prophets and judges, and they asked Him for a king. Now God was trying to reveal the future of His children with the coming of a kingdom, but because of their blindness and the depravity still in their souls, He performed powerful miracles by His Spirit before their eyes to demonstrate that He has not only the power but also the authority to back up His claims as their God. Words without a power base behind them will only be words. Therefore, these acts were also a show of His undeniable love, trust, and commitment to them. Over time, man's free will crops up to defy God, distorting his thoughts and intentions, driving a wedge between what God wants and mans personal desires.

The Ten Commandments and the mitzvot

An example of this is God giving His people the Ten Commandments. These were to be their visual governing principles to guide them in their obedience to God and each other. The first five showed how they were to treat Him, and the second five were directed toward how to treat each other. God knew the provisioning of these laws could not fix their problems, but it was established as a mirror to show them when they erred, a precursor to their future need for a Savior.

To make this clearer, think about when you look into a mirror. The mirror exposes the fact that you may not have washed your whole face, as it is showing slobber on your cheeks. But the mirror only exposes a problem—it cannot fix it. That is what the law does, it exposes. So, the law reflected man's behaviours, but something more was needed to repair the problem.

Years down the road, a faction of God's chosen leaders, the rabbis, thought it would be good to add another 613 ordinances, called the mitzvot. Those 613 additional ordinances were not just made-up laws, but rather good deeds or commandments of the law that every Jewish person should adhere to, a compilation of the first five books of the Bible. In those books, God outlined how His people should carry themselves: various dietary laws, business dealings, handling the poor, festivals and feasts, prophecy, etc.. Adding to what He had already written was one of the major missteps of God's chosen leaders, as they would later find they opened the door for confusion. Their intentions were good, but not initiated by God. Note, God did not keep them from implementing their plans. He remained focused on His plan.

Prophets and kings

In tandem with all of this, God also established the prophets more prominently as His spokespersons. After the fall, His Spirit was no longer in man, but now the manner in which the Spirit would manifest Himself was to come upon man, endowing him with a voice to speak God's words and to do special miracles. These were not just any words but words of what was to come, what direction to take, how to prepare, along with various signs and wonders. The things they spoke and manifested were of things they had no physical knowledge of nor could perform without the Holy Spirit's divine instruction and intervention. Again, this was another measure to prove His nature and character among His people. He also set up judges to govern over them accordingly. This is all a part of the establishing of His governmental blueprint.

Their adherence to His structure would provide victory and relief from any ills a society would have, but it would require one thing: submission. God, being very patient, spent many years demonstrating to His chosen people His consistency and their inability to trust Him. This governing process was not a dictatorship, a democracy, or a republic, but rather the sovereign rule of His kingship. Their free will was still intact, giving them the autonomy to follow or disobey the words of His prophets.

Another example of the people altering God's blueprint is when they desired a physical king, a person to be named leader over them, so they went to the prophet and made their request known. Scripture tells us that this request was a result of them looking around at other kingdoms that had visible kings and wanting to look like them. This was a serious request, as it resembled what Adam did in the garden. This was another act of treason by the chosen people of God. This time, man did not entertain another voice; rather, he requested another man, presumably one who could be led by God and fulfill their desire to look like everyone else. They did not see it as a rejection of God but an enhancement to what He already established, just like they did when they added 613 more laws to the Ten Commandments. Again, this was not God's blueprint, but He acquiesced because His plan was going to prevail.

God also gave revelation to the prophets about the purpose for the blueprint of the kingdom. Abraham, Moses, Samuel, David, Isaiah, Zachariah, and others all spoke of a kingdom that was to come. Isaiah summed it up more succinctly when he spoke in Isaiah 9:6, *"For unto to us a child is born, unto us a son is given, and the government shall be upon his shoulder...."* (See appendix IV for more scriptural references.) This government is in reference to the kingdom of God. Again, God provided the message, but somehow the desires of the religious rulers eclipsed His original intent, as they had their eyes set on a king who would represent them . Oh, how we still see this today. This is why the scriptures say to walk by faith and not by sight. What we see through our physical eyes will distort what God has placed in our spiritual heart. We must remember that we are spiritual beings having an earthly experience, not human beings having a spiritual experience. Until we learn this, our actions will lead to our demise, delays, and/or our potential withdrawal from God.

Our plans versus God's plans

I mention these three instances of rebellion, and there were many others, to provide clarity about what it means to follow Jesus with all our heart, soul and mind. Our plans, no matter how noble and helpful they may seem, will always come up short against His perfect plans. We are not on the same level and therefore not in a position to tweak, twist, nip, clip, or modify what the God of the universe has already said. Our human intentions, although they are good ideas, will alter our path toward obtaining His intended results for our life. It's like shooting a basketball into a hoop: a correct shot must have the right trajectory on it and be aimed at the basket so that it will go above the rim and into the net with the right velocity. Without that trajectory, the same motion of a shot will either hit the rim or totally miss it, resulting in missing the intended goal. For believers today, it's not good enough to just shoot the shot at the basket, we need to make the goal as He intends so we don't miss his mark.

Through their many failures and successes, wins and losses, disappointments and discouragements, His chosen people continued to wrestle with His blueprint. Was this because God's standards and expectations were too high, or was it to demonstrate to us today that man was always deficient and devoid of His ability to meet God's standard on his own? This is not a failure of God, but rather a part of His plan still unfolding for mankind.

John the Baptist challenges the old school

After a period of 400 years with no messages from the prophets, the next prophet the people heard from was John the Baptist. At this point, God's children were fully steeped into their religion and traditions following their revisions of His blueprint. When they encountered John the Baptist, he came preaching what was perceived as a new school of thought. Schools of thought were normal during that time. They are defined as someone who has an expert philosophy on a given subject matter and teaches with the intent to obtain followers. Plato, Socrates, and Aristotle are examples of Greek philosophers who had schools of thought. The school of thought that John the Baptist was preaching was of the kingdom of God. We know that John's role was to prepare the way for Jesus, who was the coming King that the prophets of the Old Testament preached about. The problem for the Jewish leaders was that they saw John's school of thought as being in opposition to the kingdom they were looking for. John was calling the people to repent, to change their minds by being cleansed through baptism from the bondage of sin and religious rituals taxed upon them by their religious leaders so they could enter into a life of freedom.

This concept of repenting and baptism outraged the Jewish leaders because they saw John's message as a threat to their school of thought, which focused on Abraham as their father and Moses as their law-giver. With that in mind, their school also taught them that they had no sin and therefore no need of repentance or ritual washing to make them clean. They felt that as a people, they were already cleansed through their rituals, celebrations, and festivals, as well as by their annual day of atonement where the priest went in before God and absolved them of all their wrongs. So, this baptism, cleansing, and confessions went in defiance of their standards. What they did not understand is that the repentance, confession, and baptism John represented shifted from the priest absolving everyone from their sin by his acts to every individual now needing to take personally responsibility for their sin and cleansing.

The prophets had spoken accurately concerning a coming King with His kingdom, but the interpretation was distorted by the religious leaders. They had manifested their own version of the assignment of the coming King. They altered the specifications of the blueprint that had been laid down by the prophets. It's like looking at a blueprint and not validating the dimensions so that when the door arrives, it does not fit the frame. At this point, you have two choices: to suck up your pride, admit the mistake, and correct it, or to alter the blueprint to fit the door. If the latter is chosen, it will throw off all the other dimensions of the building and it will not be fit for its proper use. This can happen to us today as well, when we find ourselves in oppressive situations and we develop the most suitable and sensible remedy for our situation.

Because it is plausible, and bolsters agreement with our peers, family, friends, etc., we pursue it whole-heartedly, only to find out that we made some wrong assumptions and now our reputation is on the line. Instead of reviewing the prophets' messages, the religious leaders stuck with their version of the King they wanted to see and missed their visitation. Their philosophy of being in bondage or under the control of another kingdom was never their understanding, as they were God's chosen. They even argued with

Jesus about this later in John 8:33-44, when Jesus told them that He had come to set them free. It became obvious that they did not know they needed to be redeemed, restored, and saved. God's picture was a much grander and more robust plan that would free everyone from their spiritual bondage, despite their ignorance of it, and restore peace between God and man, but they had to repent to obtain it.

Are we, too, missing His message?

It was now time for God to take the next step to bring forth the fleshly embodiment of His original blueprint from (Gen 1:26) and reinforce it to His people, His message revealing the true access point, the door of entry, that everyone must go through to get back to the Father. As the scripture says in Matthew 13:15, *"For this people's heart is waxed gross, and their ears are dull of hearing, and their eyes they have closed; lest at any time they should see with their eyes and hear with their ears, and should understand with their heart, and should be converted, and I should heal them."* Often, we get locked into pride, which keeps us from advancing because we don't want to be wrong or go against the crowd. We want to keep the status quo because it is easier. So, His chosen people still sit today, believing that this concept of repentance to gain access to this kingdom is absurd, and thereby delaying their own personal freedom.

Here's the point I'm making in this chapter: just as God's chosen people thought they were in alignment with His plan, we, the church, are not exempt from being in error either. Our personal belief systems can become a catalyst for our personal thoughts and opinions about how we want things to be, as opposed to what they were meant to be by our Creator. I would like you to consider a parallel between the religious leaders of God's chosen people and the Christian church's divisions today. We know that in the Old Testament, the religious leaders broke off from each other and created religious sects that catered to their liking, such as the Pharisees, Sadducees, Essenes, Herodians, and Zealots. Each of these sects believed in the same coming King and attracted people to their schools of thought based on their own ideologies and philosophies about how the King would operate. With that in mind, today's church reveals the same type of structure with our different denominations, as we too are believing in the same King and yet having different ideologies and philosophies concerning what He wants from us. Did you know that according to the Center for the Study of Global Christianity, "Estimations show there are more than 200 Christian denominations in the U.S. and a staggering 45,000 globally"?[7] Moreover that there are "10,000 distinct religions in the world"[8]. Things that make you say "Hmm."

We need to be mindful of the fact that God does not override our free will, yet just because He is not zapping us into submission does not mean that He agrees with our assessment and/or representation of His kingdom plan. Free will is a paradox because it implies self-governance, but I believe God's objective in giving us free choice was for us to freely choose Him to govern over us.

CHAPTER 5

THE GOSPEL

So, what is the gospel message? In Webster's 1828 Dictionary, "gospel is defined as "the history of the birth, life, actions, death, resurrection, ascension and doctrines of Jesus Christ: or the grace of God to fallen man through a mediator, including the character, actions, and doctrines of Christ and his apostles. This gospel is said to have been preached to Abraham, by the promise 'in thee shall the nations be blessed.'"[9] The first mention we hear of this word was at the birth of Jesus from one of heaven's messengers, the angel Gabriel, who appeared to some shepherds in Luke 2:10-11: *"And the angel said unto them, Fear not: for, behold, I bring you good tidings of great joy, which shall be to all people. For unto you is born this day in the city of David a Savior, which is Christ the Lord."*

Jesus was that good news. God's commission had now brought heaven to earth to fulfil His original plan: His plan to restore His kingdom by way of redemption of man, recovery through His resurrection, resulting in reconciliation between God and man. God would remain in heaven, and His son Jesus would be in the earth taking on flesh to be a walking representation of what Adam was designed to do, ruling and reigning.

As you have just read, the message of the gospel has many layers. Throughout the New Testament, it is referred to as the gospel, the gospel of the kingdom, the gospel of Jesus, the gospel of God, the gospel of grace, and the gospel of Christ, all tying together multiple facets of the kingdom of God. The first layer or the foundation of the gospel is the restoration of the kingdom of God that Adam lost in the garden. Without that restoration, there is nothing to build upon, as that loss precipitated the need for man's salvation through Jesus as well as the return of the Holy Spirit in man. Jesus' role embodies the totality of this gospel message of restoration, redemption, regeneration, recovery, and rebirth between humanity and God.

With multiple layers of the gospel, it is a curious thing how this message is preached. If we lose sight of the entirety of what the kingdom has to offer, then we can minimize important factors surrounding its overarching implications. What am I saying is, most often when the message of the gospel is presented, it is in regard to salvation. The message of salvation is the provision for us to be delivered from our enemies, to convert us from darkness to light, and to reconcile us back to the Father. I am not saying that salvation is not significant; rather I am suggesting that there are other facets of the kingdom that we don't focus on too much because Sunday morning is not enough time. In Isaiah 9:6, we are told that Jesus would bear the government upon His shoulders, i.e., the entirety of the kingdom of the sovereign God. Salvation is not a government. Salvation is the way to come under the governmental structure that Jesus would be putting into place. You may think this is just semantics, but I will show you as we continue.

I pose a question for you today. If Adam had not sinned, would we have needed a Savior? I would say no. Jesus was the insurance policy God established from the beginning to ensure that if man would not follow His commands, He would still be able to fulfil His plan to extend heaven to earth with His creation. I don't presume that followers of Christ have been taught to see it this way. Please hear me, I am not saying that Jesus did not need to come to the earth to die for man, I am speaking of looking at what His role would have been if Adam had not sinned. What I am outlining here is for us to look at what God's original plan for man was. The roles we know Jesus did fulfil as a prophet, king, and high priest were all after sin, but He was born of God before the earth was, to be that insurance for the Father's plan to be manifested. Nevertheless, when man did rebel, it thrust Jesus into position for the role of Savior. To accomplish this, He would have to take on human flesh as a man to reverse the penalty for sin so the kingdom of God could be reestablished on the earth. This is the gospel of Jesus Christ, the good news of the kingdom of God.

The two roles of Jesus

Jesus laid the foundation for the reestablishment of the gospel of the kingdom, through His birth, death, burial, and resurrection. He fulfilled it in the two roles he was given according to scripture:

one as the Son of Man (Luke 19:10), and the other as the Son of God (1 John 3:8). As the Son of Man, He put on flesh to pay the spiritual penalty for sin so eternal death would no longer reign over humanity. As the Son of God, He was to exercise His power and authority over Satan to annihilate his kingdom, the kingdom of darkness, rule over mankind. The paradox of His work was that humanity did not know that we needed saving. They thought their oppressor was the Romans. Today the unsaved think they have no oppressor and are not under any type of bondage. This darkness has passed down humanity's genealogy since Adam, and that proves that spiritual Stockholm Syndrome is still alive and well in the earth. This is the beauty of that scripture that Paul writes in Romans 5:8: *"But God commendeth his love toward us, in that, while we were yet sinners, Christ died for us."* This was the ultimate expression of His love for us, to come and rescue humanity from Satan's enslavement even though we were not aware of it. For those who are believers of Jesus, if you trace back in your life and recall a time when you were not looking for Jesus, you would not have considered yourself lost or enslaved. It was not until you heard the gospel message of the kingdom that you realized you were not complete. In (John 15:16) Jesus reminds us, *"Ye have not choose me, but I chose you...."* He came for us!

The births of both Adam and Jesus were miraculous, as neither of them were conceived by conventional means, Adam being handmade by God and Jesus by the Holy Spirit. This is why Jesus could be called the last Adam. He would do what the first Adam could not by fully obeying the command of the Father, even to His death. Jesus would now be the earthly model of the finished product God desired for man to emulate in the earth through the restoration of the kingdom of God. This is where I feel we drop off in our teaching about the kingdom of God. When we see or here of Jesus our thoughts go immediately to the cross and our salvation and the miraculous He performed while on earth. However, those miraculous events were not only show off His power as God but to show his future kingdom citizens that the same power He has they will have (Luke 10:19). This power, healing the sick, walking on water, raising the dead, casting out devils etc., is the restoration of what Adam originally lost in the garden. Jesus gave us live demonstrations of what He wanted to see in the future from his kingdom citizens. It appears that somewhere in our Christian denominations this understanding has not been totally accepted or adopted. These actions were not to put Him in a class all by himself rather to show us that this is now the class of kingdom citizens. Beyond Jesus' role of saviour, He was not sent to earth just to be an anomaly but to embody the prototype the Father desired in Adam.

Jesus' message: the gospel of the kingdom

As soon as Jesus was baptized by John, the scripture tells us in Matthew 4:17, *"From that time Jesus began to preach, and to say, Repent: for the kingdom of heaven is at hand."* (See appendix V for more scriptural references.) Here, He was echoing the exact same words that John the Baptist had been preaching in his school of thought. Additionally, after His resurrection, the last words he spoke to His apostles were teaching them things pertaining to the kingdom (Acts 1:28). Notice that the focus was not Him or His name, which is powerful and beneficial to all believers; the central message that was to be preached was the kingdom. It is apparent that His apostles got that message and passed it down, as the Apostle Paul, who did not walk with Jesus on the earth, has passages that state he was preaching the kingdom of God as well as other Apostles. (See appendix VI for more scriptural references.)

It is the message of the kingdom of God that Jesus was commissioned to preach, which was to restore humanity's connection and dominion authority that Adam had lost. The life Adam had in the garden did not require salvation, only relationship and adherence to his Creator. Dr. Myles Munroe put it very succinctly: "A kingdom is the governing influence of a king over his territory, impacting it with his will, his purpose, and his intent."[10] That is a mouthful but provides a clear definition as to what God's original plan was and how Jesus' role would facilitate this process. Additionally, this too helps us know that Jesus came for more than just our salvation.

One may say that this is just semantics, as Jesus and the kingdom are one. This is true; however, while the messaging we hear from the pulpits emphasizes the need for salvation to get to heaven, which is important, however what Jesus spent his time preaching was not heaven, but the kingdom of God and it's operation on the earth. Jesus was after a product from mankind to fulfil the original mandate of Adam in the garden, to have dominion over the earth, to reproduce and multiply etc. Let me say it this way: it is one thing to purchase a ticket for your intended destination and another thing to get your bags packed, time your departure to the airport, drive or be driven to the airport, navigate through the airport and get to your gate on time and board the plane to get to your intended destination. It appears to me that we have made the destination the ultimate plan and placed little emphasis on the process of getting there.

Don't get me wrong—I am not coming down on what the Christian church is preaching, per se, rather diving into the nitty gritty of how the kingdom message is packaged. I say this because I sense there are more people who are drawn to salvation that leads to the promises of the contents or blessings of its byproducts, namely heaven, when the byproducts of the kingdom of God are much more comprehensive and ask for our compliance to adhere to its governing principles to attain God's fulfilment for His children's lives. Our salvation is just the tip of the iceberg. There is more life and purpose to be found between our salvation and our destination in heaven.

God's government is a surer thing than the governments in the natural world from which we seek things. This is why Jesus clearly tells us in Matthew 6:33 to seek first the kingdom of God and His righteousness and all these things will be added. We often forget the "and" in that verse, which ties the kingdom to adhering to His governance, His way of doing and being. Preaching the totality of the kingdom is the first priority, meaning that when you get the kingdom, you get the king and all He has to offer. It may be all semantics, but when getting to heaven is the driving force of the salvation message, we lose sight of the entirety of Jesus' purpose in the earth—those things we spoke of earlier, the restoration of everything Adam had lost. Adam lost his connection to eternal life with the Father, he lost the connection with the Holy Spirit, and he lost the kingdom dominion and authority he was given. Salvation was not Jesus' main emphasis, it was the restoration of the kingdom of God's operation in the earth of which salvation was the catalyst to facilitate it.

Just to drive this point further, when our primary focus on the kingdom is reduced to the message of salvation, we miss other parts of the kingdom that relate to our lives after salvation. Those things of the kingdom I will call byproducts. Byproducts are a result of something created out of the original thing that was created—basically, a secondary product or offshoot from the original. For example, the byproducts of a cow are steaks, ground beef, beef ribs, milk, etc. These secondary products are delicious to some, but they cannot represent the cow in its totality, and at the same time, they cannot be excluded from it either. This is how the gospel of the kingdom should be viewed. The kingdom is the lifestyle, our overarching governance for life, with Jesus being our King and us being His citizens. It is the principal operation of the King that has been gifted to His creation.

The byproducts of becoming a part of this lifestyle are what Jesus displayed as He walked the earth. He went around healing, delivering, setting people free, and showing them how to communicate with one another as well as with the Father. He showed us how to overcome adversity, how to forgive, how to be selfless in our giving. He did not preach prosperity, but rather financial principles that would produce in and for His kingdom. All of these byproducts were available to those who would choose to accept Him as the door to the kingdom. These actions proved that He was the door, as He stated in John 10:9. Thinking critically, that means He is the gateway to something more than we currently have, because doors take us to things and through things, as well as shut in and close off things.

How we're getting it wrong today

Maybe we should reconsider preaching as Jesus did concerning the kingdom. He was not concerned about the title of His follower rather their adoption of the kingdom He was representing before them. As a side note, when Jesus was on the earth, His followers were referred to as people of "the way," which came from His declaration of being the way, the truth, and the life in John 14:6. Even before Saul converted to Paul, he was trying to kill the people of "the way," not Christians (Acts 9:2).

It was the pagans in Antioch who called Jesus' followers Christians (Acts 11:26). Is it possible that the early church leaders took on the name "Christians" from the pagans so they could have an official title as a community? I mean, we have the Greek, Roman, and Egyptian gods that had names for their followers, whereas the Christians were "the people of the way." I am not taking away the significance of the name we call ourselves, Christians, but rather how we obtained this adoption of said name. Could it be that the people of the way wanted a name for their religion that would stand up against the names of the other deities of the time? This kind of smells like what the religious Jews did when they asked God for a king so they could look like everyone else. God allowed it, just as He did in the New Testament even though Jesus never used the word "Christian." Food for thought, remembering God is on a mission to establish His world, His purpose, and His plan.

In my opinion, much of what I hear in our pulpits today is preaching the byproducts or benefits of the kingdom. Benefits are great; however, when the focus is "you will get this if you do that," this was not what Jesus preached. We appeal to the world's desire for what we think is "the good life" here on earth more than the eternal life, which is the best life. The release from the maladies of life is a vital part of the equation, but it does not fully explain the value of a relationship with Jesus and His kingdom. The world we live in is more about what we can get than what we can give. This means that if I can speak a message that will get someone what they desire in the now, they will be bought in but not understanding the right reasons. This message of instant, visible gratification is not the gospel that Jesus preached to draw people into His kingdom.

What I am saying here is that the impacts of the kingdom, these byproducts, must be preached within the context of how a king operates within His kingdom construct. I know I am painting a broad brush, but if I were to guess, those who are attending churches today are mostly current believers, especially in these post-pandemic years. People are clamoring for messages from pulpits, on podcasts, and all the other social media formats in hopes of finding an easy way to obtain whatever they are desiring. We must be cautious of the packaging of our messages. As preachers and teachers, our job is to preach the total kingdom operation, not our best appeal or gimmick to attract people to our congregations. I don't believe that any preacher of the gospel intends to shortchange the gospel message, but I have also seen that many of us just repeat what we have heard and/or seen as effective. The sad reality is that the average Christian who has been in church for years has no idea of their purpose in life or that Jesus has a purpose for their life. So one has to ask themselves, what are we preaching. Part of the kingdom message is understanding the new identity we have been given that we did not know we lost. The significance of that identity in Christ sets the stage for us to find our purpose, but somewhere, we got lost. You may not believe me, but I would ask you to take a personal survey of your friends and family who say they are saved and ask them what their purpose in life is, outside of going to heaven.

Becoming kingdom minded

It is a must that we go back and study His kingdom and ask the Holy Spirit how we can reengage our minds to become more kingdom minded in our messaging, ensuring that we are not retarding the gospel of the kingdom with inspirational sermons. We must outline the full package of the restoration of power and authority, the ability to rule and reign by dominating the earth and finding and fulfilling our purpose for being. Until this happens, the church will not be as effective in dominating the earth as intended. Below, I have gathered some perspectives on what most humans desire and how we should teach them in the context of the kingdom.

- Everyman desires healing inside or outside of the kingdom; however, God appropriated healing in the kingdom for believers to be able to fulfil the purpose He appointed for their lives, not just for prolonging sake. (Isaiah 53:5; 1 Peter 2:24)

- Everyman wants prosperity inside and outside of the kingdom; however, in the kingdom, prosperity is a commonwealth system where we ask for what we need and it will be disbursed to us for the fulfilment of His plans in the earth. As king he will appropriate in His

- time to us, not to build our own personal empire but His kingdom. (Deuteronomy 8:18)

- Everyman desires love inside and outside of the kingdom; however, the love appropriated in the kingdom has obligations. Jesus said, *"If ye love me, keep my commandments."* Additionally, kingdom love convicts and converts but does not condone our behaviour. Saul was killing the very people Jesus died for, and yet He still loved him and revealed Himself to him for the service to the kingdom. Never did He condone Saul's actions, but Saul was converted by the love and forgiveness He received from Jesus when he was confronted with the actions he thought was right in his eyes but went against the principles of the kingdom. (John 14:15, 16:8)

- Everyman desires grace, or a second chance inside and outside of the kingdom; however, grace in the kingdom was granted to man as God's divine ability and influence upon man for him to carry out His purpose. Grace is an empowerment, not a covering for sin.(Rom 5:21)

- Everyman desires to have giftings inside and outside of the kingdom; however, in the kingdom, they are to be used to display the nature and character of God as He wills. (1 Corinthians 12:11)

- Everyman desires peace inside and outside of the kingdom; however, peace is not the absence of war, but rather the absence of inner conflict and fear when trouble arises. (John 14:27)

- Everyman desires safety inside and outside of the kingdom; however, true safety can only be found in the King of the Kingdom, Jesus. (Psalm 91:1)

- Everyman desires trust inside and outside of the kingdom; however, trust can only be found in God's truth. (Proverbs 3:5-6)

- Everyman desires to have faith inside and outside of the kingdom; however, while the world calls it manifesting their desires, faith was never to be used outside of the kingdom of God, because it is the only thing that the scripture says pleases Him. (Hebrews 11:6)

- Lastly, everyman inside and outside of the kingdom desires to have a government that is just in all their deeds, a great counsellor, equitable in the distribution their power and might, always available, and to provide peace. All these character traits are fulfilled in Jesus, the king of the kingdom. (Isaiah 9:6)

In my first book, *From Faith to Faith: The Faith That Separates God from Other god's*, I spell out what faith is by way of an acronym: Full Assurance in the Holy Ghost. Utilizing that expression separates the kingdom of God from other gods, as no other religion has a Holy Ghost. Faith is kingdom language. By the way, it is only by faith that the gospel of the kingdom can be carried out, because faith is the currency of heaven.

So, we can summarize this chapter with Jesus' last words on the cross, *"It is finished"* (John 19:30). What was His finished work on the earth? It was the restoration of the path from earth to heaven, the reestablishment of communication between man and the Father, and the release of the deposit of the Holy Spirit in the earth through man to to fulfil his destiny. Before His departure, Jesus told His apostles that the Father would be commissioning the Holy Spirit back into the earth realm. This meant the mobilization and globalization of the message of the kingdom to take flight into all the earth by the Holy Spirit.

Part III:

HIS PLAN – The Holy Spirit

CHAPTER 6

GOD'S RENOVATION PLAN FOR MAN

Now that Jesus has paved the way for us to get back to the Father, the renovation of the mind of man is now in force. Our salvation was a spiritual transaction, just as Adam's treason in the garden was. In these transactions, there was nothing we could touch, see, or feel that let us know about our new condition and status. With Adam, death became our spiritual default setting, and through Jesus' death, burial, and resurrection, we obtained eternal life by faith. Our confession of faith made us right with God again, but it did not convert our soul. We were delivered from the power of God's enemies that had taken up residence in our soul. We were purged from the guilty stain of sin by His blood, but our conscience was still attached to the habits, appetites, and desires from our old nature. In order to exchange that old nature, it requires understanding of our new kingdom. Jesus spent a lot of time providing us with earthly examples of kingdom life. His examples gave us a glimpse of the life that has been restored to us. He was not showing us anything new, but rather exposing to us what Adam originally had access to before his sin. With Jesus having reactivated His deposit into man, the Spirit of God is now accessible for the next phase of the Father's plan: the gift of the Holy Ghost.

Before we step fully into His role, let's talk about gifts for a moment. In our society, we have become so self-absorbed that we want to know what our gift is before we get it. We make lists to ensure that our request is made known. If the gift given is not what we want, one of four things will occur: we will regift it, leave it unopened, open it and not use it, or open and possibly misuse it. In the kingdom of God, His citizens are given gifts. These gifts are given freely—the gift of the Holy Spirit, the gift of righteousness, the gift of grace, the gift of God, and the gift of Christ—and now it is up to us to open and explore them. We must be careful not to overlook them or think we have all we need, as they all provide an important role and operation in our kingdom life.

The acceptance of our salvation is not the end of our faith, it is only the beginning. Through our faith, we have crossed a great chasm to believe in a man we have not seen to take us to a place we have not been, and to believe He will come back for us. We must know that once we have made that leap, our work for the kingdom begins. I feel like religion has caused believers to stop short of seeing the importance of all the gifts God has appropriated to His citizens. We need every one of them to complete our personal renovation to the original mandate God has for his kingdom.

For example, prior to our salvation, you might say we were a condemned building, and after our salvation, we gained the proper building permits to make the required renovations, i.e., the Holy Spirit. Remember, renovation is not a demolishing of the old building, but rather a transformation or a repurposing, or, better stated, a restoration of said building. What I am saying here is that if we don't submit to the renovation, we will not pass the building inspection at the appointed time of completion; the building will never reach its potential and will therefore become an eyesore to the community. These gifts came down from heaven and are available to those who answer the call to Christ. This is what Jesus was trying to explain to Nicodemus.

Jesus' enlightenment of Nicodemus

This process of renovation can be traced back to a strategic encounter that Jesus had with the highest teacher of the law, a Pharisee, named Nicodemus. He was a religious leader of the Jews and held in high regard among the Sanhedrin council. His superiority of the interpretation of the law, the blueprint the children of Israel had been given, was revered by all. However, with this great knowledge, he had become perplexed at what he saw in Jesus, who, at a young age, effortlessly spoke and performed miracles not following the blueprint Moses had laid down.

What Jesus told Nicodemus in that conversation demonstrates God's plan for all men. The first thing Jesus said was that one must be born again "to see" the kingdom of God. What does that mean? Man must acknowledge and accept Jesus as Lord and Savior, that spiritual transaction we just talked about. Without that, man has no physical means to see or understand the kingdom of God at work. For example, when a person witnesses or has been part of something that should have had a catastrophic outcome, but the person survived, a non-believer would say that it was luck, while a believer would say God's angels protected the person. One cannot see or speak to God at work in any instance if they don't believe, so the nonbeliever refers to the situation as lucky.

Secondly, Jesus told him that one must be born of water and the Spirit in order "to enter" into the kingdom of God. In a natural birth, the baby first sits in darkness in the womb of their mother for the determined amount of time. In that place, everything is opaque and dark, but there will come a time when the baby goes through a transition of a new birth into another realm they have never experienced before. When they awaken into their new realm, they are washed off and cleansed from the watery grave they were in and are now exposed to the light, where they have freedoms they have never known. They can walk, talk, run, jump, learn, etc. Now their new life has just begun. A spiritual birth come from our confession of faith in Jesus Christ. In that instance the Holy Spirit becomes alive in our consciousness. He is referred to as the living water (John 7:38). His activation in our lives is the power that will enable us to become effective kingdom citizens.

The conclusion of this matter is that we must be reborn into the kingdom of God. The first time we were born in the earth, God breathed into man without his consent to bring him to life, and man became a living soul (Genesis 2:7). Now, by way of Jesus, He requires man's consent for His entry into His life (Romans 10:9).

Work out your soul salvation

So, what do we do with our salvation? Is our confession of faith the end of the job for the kingdom citizen? Do we just sit back and try to be the best person we can be until Jesus returns for us? Is our job just to work on sinning less? What is the plan for man after salvation?

The Apostle Paul tells us in Philippians 2:12 to work out our soul salvation. That work is defined as to accomplish, achieve, and perform. Performance here is not in a sense of earning through our acts but of fulfilling the original mandate given by God with direction from the Holy Spirit. This is why the kingdom message is so important, as there is a mission on the other side of our salvation. I am not saying we work for it; you cannot work for something you already have. What I am saying is that it was a free gift, and our responsibility now is to work at it, i.e., to accomplish and achieve it. It's just like marriage: you don't work for marriage, you work at it once you have gone through the ceremony. As stated earlier, the ultimate goal of the Holy Spirit in God's plan is for man to reveal God's kingdom in the earth. Think of it this way: the Holy Spirit is now the agent responsible for the rollout of the first mobility plan to reestablish the kingdom of God in the earth through man.

This is why we were called to repentance, a change of mind from our old life under Satan's kingdom. We must change. Salvation was a spiritual transaction, and now the transformation or renovation must reestablish the foundation in our natural mind so His Spirit and our flesh will agree. Our repentance is not defined by an emotional outburst at the church altar. That is called godly sorrow. Repentance is a change of our heart, a 180-degree turn, leaving the old to go to the new. This is the heart transplant that God revealed to the prophet Ezekiel in Ezekiel 36:26-27:

> *A new heart also will I give you, and a new spirit will I put within you: and I will take away the stony heart out of your flesh, and I will give you an heart of flesh. And I will put my spirit within you, and cause you to walk in my statutes, and ye shall keep my judgments, and do them.*

The acceptance of this spiritual heart transplant has given us another opportunity to live the life we were intended to live. Now, the work of the Holy Spirit in man begins and ends with our conversion. The Spirit of God has now been activated. Whe Jesus disciples asked him how to pray his response was found in Matthew 6:9-10, "Our father which art in heaven, hallowed by they name. Thy kingdom come, thy will be done, in earth as it is in heaven". These are not words of a religious prayer only for Christians; it was Jesus telling his disciples that the kingdom was open to all men because he is the father of mankind. It is called the Lord's prayer because it was a call of the kingdom to all humanity.

How can His kingdom come or His will be done if Jesus does not have people to reproduce the kingdom life on earth? We know that after Jesus ascended to heaven, the Apostles carried on His mission, and this is what the Apostle Peter said to new believers about their conversion. Acts 3:17-21 (AMP) says:

> *Now, brothers, I know that you acted in ignorance [not fully aware of what you were doing], just as your rulers*

> *did also. And so God has fulfilled what He foretold by the mouth of all the prophets, that His Christ (Messiah, Anointed) would suffer. So **repent** [change your inner self—your old way of thinking, regret past sins] and return [to God—**seek His purpose for your life**], so that your sins may be wiped away [blotted out, completely erased], so that times of refreshing may come from the presence of the Lord [restoring you like a cool wind on a hot day].*

There are two key phrases here: "repent" and "seek His purpose for your life." "Repent" is defined as "to change ones mind,"[11] and "seek His purpose for your life" means to "turn to, to cause to return, to bring back."[12] The best word for this would be conversion or restoration. Restoration has to come through the renewal of the spirit of man's mind so that he can come into alignment with his new King and kingdom.

The challenge here is that since we were under the effects of spiritual Stockholm Syndrome, we never knew what our original life was supposed to be or the expectations of it. Our life in Christ is more than a confession; it is also an adaptation to His eternal system. I think that in our traditional teaching, we have somewhat minimized man's expectations after our salvation, focusing more on the benefits of the kingdom than on the expectations of the King. We have religious debates on what Jesus said, what He implied, what Paul said, and what Paul implied, all the while minimizing the message coming from the Holy Spirit that will lead us into all truth. This does not negate the Apostle Paul's teaching, nor that of any of the other Apostles, but the Holy Spirit has been given full authorization to bring us into all truth. It is that relationship that validates the truth, not our truth. This is where the Catholic Church has made some grave mistakes, in that they worship Mary and their rosary beads in a higher esteem than what Jesus has said. Jesus said in Matthew 11:11 *"Verily I say unto you, Among them that are born of women there hath not risen a greater than John the Baptist: notwithstanding he that is least in the kingdom of heaven is greater than he."* It is individual beliefs like these that divide or intercept the truth from what God said and make denominations that serve men and not God.

Another example of Jesus truth' is found in Luke 6:27 (AMP): *"But I say to you who hear [Me and pay attention to My words]: Love [that is, unselfishly seek the best or higher good for] your enemies, [make it a practice to] do good to those who hate you."* How many of the citizens of the kingdom of God hold this to be a true practice in their lives? If we are truthful, not many, as we allow our own sentiments to get in the way of His expectations, His truth for us. Another example is when one of Jesus' prospective followers asked Him if they could go bury their father before they followed Him. Jesus' response was *"Let the dead bury their dead"* (Luke 9:60). Again, I am sure most people would say, "That is not what Jesus meant, that's so mean." All I can say is, that is what He said. Jesus is on God's mission, not ours, and it takes our daily dying to self to properly represent the kingdom of God. No wonder Jesus said a kingdom divided cannot stand, and the church is wobbling today because we want Jesus to comply with our sentiments. It is not enough to just call ourselves Christians. It is not enough to seek out the denominations of the church traditions that we like most. It is not enough to ignore teachings from the Bible that don't resonate with us. The scriptures say, one Lord, one faith, and one baptism. It is that oneness that only comes through the Holy Spirit's operation in all our lives that we will be able to become on one accord. If we want to maintain our personal truths and not take them to the Holy Spirit for confirmation, this tells me that the church is confused, because the Holy Spirit can only speak the truth.

Who is the Holy Spirit?

I can honestly say that it was not until 30 years after I was saved that I found out there was more to the role that the Holy Spirit was to play in the life of the believer. In my formative years, before college, my introduction to the Holy Spirit was reduced to seeing a person have an emotional response and praising God loudly during the service, especially after someone sang a song that ended with them bucking and shouting around the church. The conversation surrounding that outburst was that the person had caught the Holy Spirit. During that period, I also experienced a person who spoke in tongues in the service, and she was quickly ushered out of the sanctuary. I was told that what she was doing was not of God but of the devil and that is why she was removed. So, my first impression was the Holy Spirit was wild and uncontrolled, as that was accepted behaviour, and that speaking in tongues was of the devil and not accepted behaviour in the church I attended. I was not so sure if I wanted the Holy Spirit, because neither of those activities made me feel comfortable. I had not studied the scriptures for myself but believed my pastor because he was the authority. I later came to understand that this left me with a severely impaired understanding of the purpose of the Holy Spirit.

I was not aware that He was with God from Genesis through Revelation as the power source from heaven. I did not realize that

He was the one who hovered over the waters before the earth was, who put the stars in heaven, opened the Red Sea, made the walls of Jericho fall down, and came upon the prophets of God to speak forth His words, and that He now lives in every believer to empower us to fulfill our assignment in the earth. I did not understand the true purpose as to why the scripture said that He lives in me. I did not know I had a personal assignment that He was going to help me fulfil. As far as I was concerned all I really needed was to be saved. Because of my literal nature, I only grasped that that Holy Spirit was there to be my helper in case I got into trouble. This may not be your experience, but these are things that influenced my perceptions of His role in my life.

It was not until some 10+ years later that I began to pursue for myself more knowledge pertaining to this life as a Christian. I had experienced too many conflicts in my own journey trying to live out the scriptures—what I was missing was understanding. God then facilitated a move from my hometown that I was not expecting to another state. In this move, I experienced things differently than what I had been accustomed to. Previously, I was in a mainstream denominational church, and after I moved, I tried my first non-denominational church with my son, who was five at the time. Things were going fine until at the end of the service, the pastor called people up for prayer. People began to come down to the altar, and the Pastor prayed for each one of them individually. As he did that, each person began to fall down, to what I now understand as the power of the anointing, of which I had no understanding. I had no idea what was happening. During this process, my son looked at me and whispered to me, "Mommy, are they dead?" and I said to him, "I don't know," and we swiftly left that church. So here again, my experience with understanding the purpose of the Holy Spirit was confusing, as I did not think He was helping those people who had fallen down.

All of these things eventually led me to study the Bible more to make sense of it all. In the next phase of my journey, I went to a church where the Holy Spirit had more of an emphasis. It was there that I was taught that I needed to be filled with the Holy Spirit with the evidence of speaking in tongues to give me more power. I believed and received the power, but I did not know for what purpose I was to use it. So left, to my own imagination, I said to myself, "It must be to help me sin less." I did not understand what He was truly after. It was like having a fire hose connected to the hydrant and turning on the water. The pressure of the water was too much for the hose, and it whipped it around uncontrollably. I had power, but I did not know how to wield it—a very dangerous place to be.

Nevertheless, as I learned more about the Holy Spirit, I understood that the power was to help me overcome my old nature to build my relationship with the Holy Spirit and fulfill the plan God had for me. But I did not know how to find the plan, so the best I could do at this point was to wait for Jesus to return to take me home with Him. This entire process of some 20+ years has brought me to the point of writing this book in hopes of helping others understand the purpose of how God uses the Holy Spirit to bring His citizens into purpose in His kingdom.

CHAPTER 7
Changing citizenship

The desire to change

Let's go back again to Jesus' conversation with Nicodemus, as it brings to light the dichotomy in our mind: a battle of thoughts competing in our conscious mind (the things we have seen, heard, and accepted) with our subconscious mind (the things we have seen and heard but have not accepted). Depending on the magnitude of the thoughts, we are catapulted into one of three possibilities: to reject those thoughts, to accept them, or to gain more information.

As we saw with Nicodemus, he was so intrigued in his subconscious mind that he had to take another step to see if he could accept what his conscious mind thought it knew. The pull on his heart was so strong that he risked his reputation by calling a meeting with Jesus in secret at night. Nicodemus had the desire to know but found himself unable to repent, to change his mind concerning how this new kingdom overrides the law and the prophets.

Change is hard for everyone, but what happens when we are faced with information that turns our world and existence upside down, where all our experience and knowledge is dismantled right in front of our eyes? This is the power of the gospel of the kingdom of God by the Holy Spirit tugging on our heart, convicting us, but we shrug Him off. How many people, like Nicodemus, shrugged off the call to the kingdom, and yet have no answers while holding tightly to their traditions? This is why the scriptures say that our human spirit is willing but our flesh is weak (Matthew 26:41). However, it is with the power of the Holy Spirit in us that we are empowered to take that step. He does not take the step for us. We are the hydrant and He is the water. When we attach our hose to Him and turn the valve on, He will guide and teach us so we are not aimlessly spewing all over the place. Neither Jesus nor the Holy Spirit will ever override our will.

I recall a time when I was working and moving up the corporate ladder, and I came to a place where I knew I had to make a decision about my career. At that time, I had been called to ministry and had a vital role with my church, which I was impressed to remain a part of. On my job, I was put on the fast track for management, which would increase my income, title, and respect but would require moving, as the corporate policy at that time was that you never manage people you used to work with. I was happy in my church, and I was happy about being on the fast track in my company, but one day I woke up out of my sleep and heard, "Paula, you have your ladder on the wrong building." That was the Holy Spirit. At that point, I knew that I had to turn down the opportunity. The desire for ministry, which did not pay, was much more than my desire for money, prestige of title, and things. I traded temporary treasures for His eternal purpose. It was not easy; I could have told myself that I can do ministry anywhere, but I knew that the job requirements would not be conducive to ministry because of the time commitment required. So, I followed the voice of the Lord and decided not to take the opportunity. This was pivotal, as I decided that pursuing my purpose in the kingdom was much greater.

Recredentialling

This pivot can be compared to one who decides to leave their current country to live in a foreign country. The first thing required is a change of our mind, which we talked about earlier. No one can be converted until they change their mind. What drives one person may not be what drives another. Many things can be the catalyst to get someone to consider the move, whether it be other family members residing in the foreign country, a better governmental structure, the promise of future growth, access to improved development opportunities, security, or the economy of the land, to name just a few. If you are not willing to adapt to a new culture, it will not be profitable for you. It will require you to unlearn and relearn the system and laws that govern that territory.

As I discussed earlier, the Holy Spirit is the active agent given to us as a gift to teach and guide us into the truth of who we are and our purpose. To demonstrate the role of the Holy Spirit, I will liken His function to that of the official government officer who signs off on making one an official citizen. The naturalization process to get into the United States of America states the following requirements: filling out an application for admission and obtaining the acceptance of that application; passing a written and oral test of language, which includes understanding written vocabulary; and understanding the basic governmental structure, geography, and history of the new country. Additionally, a sponsor is needed in the new home country who supports and vouches for them, and they need to submit personal biometric data and have a complete medical exam. Once all these activities are completed to satisfaction, the person is invited to a naturalization ceremony. At this ceremony, requires the citizen to turn in all the credentials associated with the old country and take an oath of allegiance to the new country. Then they are declared citizens in the new country, given a new set of identification credentials, and welcomed to all the rights and privileges. What a process.

In comparison the kingdom of God has a naturalization process if you will to obtain access into it's country. You ask, how is heaven a country? The Bible tells us that heaven is a country and Jerusalem is the heavenly city within it (Hebrews 11:10; Revelation 21:2). In further support of heaven being a country, I will show you that it has all the elements that makes it one. It has a constitution; the kingdom calls it the Bible. It has a defence system; the kingdom calls it heavenly host, angels, seraphim, cherubim, and warrior angels. It has a communication system; the kingdom refers to him as Gabriel, the chief spokesperson. It has an education system; the kingdom calls Him the Holy Spirit. It has citizens; the kingdom calls them the great cloud of witnesses, martyrs, and angels. It has a leader; the kingdom calls them God the Father, Jesus the Son, and the Holy Spirit. It has an economic system; the kingdom calls common wealth, which is disbursed at the will of the King to all who have need. Lastly, the country has a physical location; the kingdom calls it heaven. So lets start the kingdom citizen process.

The application

In the world process, before you can apply to become a citizen of the United States, you must first determine if your background meets the requirements. If accepted, then you are directed to fill out an extensive application, get photos, pay fees, submit supporting documents, etc. All of this is just to begin the process for acceptance.

In the kingdom of God, there is no application, nor a fee to be paid, only a simple acknowledgment of Jesus as Lord and Savior. In case you are wondering if anyone can just acknowledge Jesus to get into His kingdom, the answer is no. The Apostle Paul tells us that no man can say Jesus is Lord unless he is empowered by the Holy Spirit (1 Corinthians 12:3).

Passing the test

In the world process, the next step is to pass a test. This test covers basic knowledge of the new government's structure, with written, oral, and geography components. Acceptance is not based on an applicant's desire alone; they have to have *studied in advance* of their application process.

In the kingdom of God, it is only *after* our acknowledgment of Jesus that studying begins. This should be job #1 for the new

Changing Citizenship

citizen, as we came to this new country knowing very little about it. Jesus stressed the importance of studying in Matthew 6:33 when He said to seek first the kingdom of God and His righteousness and all these things will be added. To seek means to study, inquire, search for. After giving us the free gift of salvation, He wanted us to explore and unwrap that totality of what the kingdom life provides. In it, we have benefits, free gifts, but also responsibilities.

Let's talk about the benefits first. We have been given free gifts in the kingdom, whereas in the world system, we are given nothing and must pay up front, fill out applications, pass a test, show proof of identification, provide a credible source of income, be able to show a payment history, and the list goes on. These free gifts from the kingdom are there to support and fulfill our lives on the earth. What that means is that we must seek understanding of every gift this kingdom has to offer, as it is truly more than salvation, (see the beginning of this chapter about all the gifts). This is not terminology we were used to in the world, so we must get understanding.

Another thing to know about gifts is that it is great to receive them, but what happens when you don't open them? Have you ever received a gift and left it unopened, or even regifted it? You acknowledge that it was a great gesture on the part of the giver, but if you did not use it, you have denied it the power to be useful in your life. It's in your possession but sitting on the shelf unopened. We walk around upset that we cannot sleep, we're always anxious, lacking peace, never trusting, in pain physically and emotionally, and we go from doctor to doctor for answers when the gift of the Holy Spirit, which was freely given to us, has all the answers.

I had a workmate who had been with the company for 10 years, and he wore glasses. I noticed that over the 10 years, he never got a new pair of glasses. One day I said to him, "You must really like those glasses, as I have never seen you change them." He laughed and I said, "Why don't you change them?" He said, "Because I don't want to spend the money on new glasses." I said to him, "In our benefit package, we can get new glasses every year with a $120 stipend." Back then, $120 was enough to get you designer glasses. He said to me, "I did not know that." I said, "You never read your benefits?" He said no. Here he was clearly missing out on something that would have been beneficial to him, but his ignorance made his life harder.

I find it interesting that there is so much controversy about the operation of the Holy Spirit. Since He is the legal agent in the earth sent by the Father to represent Jesus, we should receive everything He has to offer us. Our indifference about His role and the gifts He disburses should be unacceptable. We should not be selective with the gifts that are more palatable to us. Are we leaning on what we have heard and not studied? Have we engaged with the Holy Spirit to confirm our understanding of those gifts? As much as we want to believe that we are right, have we truly invited Him in for clarity? The scripture says He will speak the same as Jesus spoke, so to think He is giving out separate answers or instructions to different denominations is not of God. There is something wrong with our theology when the only common theme the Christian churches can come together on is our belief that Jesus died on the cross and rose again. The rest of the book is not up for interpretation. So I ask, are we engaging the Holy Spirit to teach and guide us into *all* truth? This is His plan to have His church on one accord. Let's reread how Jesus described the role of the Holy Spirit in our lives in John 14:26:

But the comforter, which is the Holy Ghost, whom the Father will send in my name, he shall teach you all things, and bring all things to your remembrance, whatsoever I have said unto you.

The requirement for study confirms that we have more of a role after salvation than just to wait for Jesus' return. Additionally, in 2 Timothy 2:15, the scripture challenges us to study (make haste) to show ourselves approved (tried/accepted) unto God and not be ashamed, rightly dividing the word of truth. We all know what it feels like to not do well in our studies: it produces shame. This verse is telling us that if we want God's approval, we must study so we won't be ashamed.

It is our kingdom responsibility to unlearn the former habits, desires, and appetites that we came into the kingdom of God with. When we spend personal time in the scriptures, the Holy Spirit will lead us and bring revelation to our understanding so that we can operate correctly under the governance of God. Often people ask where they should start reading the Bible to get understanding. My response is that it does not matter. If there is a desire or draw to the scripture, we can trust the Holy Spirit to bring revelation and inspiration to the reader, as He knows them better than we do. It's all about our relationship with Him. The Holy Spirit is not a process but a person. He is like us having our personal Jesus physically right here with us to ask questions of.

The second component of our seeking/studying is understanding His righteousness. This was a word that I never clearly understood growing up in church. As a matter of fact, I cannot say that I heard many sermons regarding it. But in reading this scripture, how could we overlook it? I have heard the word often, and the most common definitions were to be in right standing with God or to be in right standing with the government of the kingdom of God. All those definitions translated in my mind as my need to be perfect without sin. I had no idea that it meant I was made right even though I did wrong. I kept trying to make myself right with God when He had already done it through Jesus.

This revelation blew my mind, because wrong is wrong and right is right, so how can you make wrong right? I needed to understand this government of God more fully, as this was no kind of law or government I had ever known. I honestly believe that if you ask Christians to explain righteousness in context with their current walk with God, the majority of them would not be able to clearly articulate it. Try it and see for yourself. It may be the missing ingredient as to why we are not receiving the "things" at the end of Matthew 6:33.

A key scripture that clarifies the role of righteousness in the life of a kingdom citizen is Romans 1:16-17: *"For I am not ashamed of the gospel of Christ: for it is the power of God unto salvation to every one that believeth; to the Jew first, and also to the Greek. For therein is the righteousness of God revealed from faith to faith: as it is written, The just shall live by faith."* This scripture is telling us that the power of the gospel, the resurrection of Jesus that we received by faith, is the same power that makes us right with God, and we must live by that principle. This is kingdom, supernatural revelation. It does not equate with our natural understanding. This is why we must study! We are now citizens of a heavenly country that does not operate using earthly principles. The Bible is a supernatural book and was never intended for us to be able to relate to it with our natural mind, but only through the mind of Christ, which the Holy Spirit reveals to us. This is a conundrum for our natural minds.

This is where our faith comes in. The world system does not operate on faith, it operates on physical proof. As citizens, we must know that faith is the currency of heaven. Since heaven is our home country that never runs out of resources and we live in another country that has limitations, we use our faith to pull in resources from our home country, so we are not insufficient in anything. It is our operation of faith that pleases God (Hebrews 11:6), not our church attendance, nor our financial contributions, nor giving to the poor, nor sacrificing our time working in the ministry. Faith is our having full assurance in the Holy Spirit that He will provide us the direction, wisdom, guidance, and provision as we work with Him.

Another capstone of what righteousness can be is found in Romans 14:17: *"For the kingdom of God is not meat and drink; but righteousness, and peace, and joy in the Holy Ghost."* When we are in right standing (compliance) with God's government, we can be at peace and have joy. It's all about being in alignment, but within His standards that the Holy Spirit guides us into. Our problem is that we make our own laws, our own truth that we abide by and falsely believe that Jesus sanctions it because it makes sense to us. But we are not the creator of the world—this is not about our plan or our purpose. We must be true to His words, as it is only the boundaries He has set for man that will give us our best life. An entire book can be written on this subject, but I will leave that to you to pursue with the Holy Spirit.

Lastly, with study, there are tests. These tests are similar to how God proved or proofed the children of Israel as they were developing their relationship with Him in the Old Testament. That proofing was God testing their faith in His leadership as directed through His leaders. These tests are still alive and well for the New Testament believer. As the scripture says, the trying of our faith works patience (James 1:2-3). That word "trying" is defined as testing. This testing is not about passing or failing, but rather our allegiance to Him.

We must learn the constitution, the governing principles that have been established to be productive citizens. Remember the model prayer Jesus spoke to the disciples when they asked Him to teach them how to pray. He told them to pray like this: *"thy kingdom come, thy will be done on earth as it is in heaven"* (Matthew 6:10). I must say that in my early walk with Jesus, I thought the statement "thy kingdom come" was asking Jesus to get back here and come and take us home. Additionally, I thought that "thy will be done" was talking about me not sinning as opposed to me fulfilling the purpose He has for me while I'm in the earth. It never crossed my mind that God had a specific purpose for me in the earth, so my plan was to be the best person I could by not sinning against Him and wait for His return to go to heaven. That was it. I thought my purpose was to find Jesus, and I had found Him. I knew that I was supposed to stop sinning, but I was more focused on not doing wrong, and trying to make myself be right, when Jesus already took care of it.

Finding a sponsor

The requirement for a sponsor in the naturalization process in the US requires that the sponsor be a US citizen, have a residence, meet an income requirement, and sign an affidavit that legally binds them to take on financial responsibility to support the candidate until their application is approved.

In the kingdom of God, the Holy Spirit is our sponsor. He was delegated to supply all the power and authority needed in our new kingdom. We can't restore ourselves, because we don't know the original design. We were born in sin. We were enslaved by a different master. This is where the Holy Ghost comes in to help us mature; as the Apostle Paul spoke in Hebrews 6:1, we must move beyond the elementary teachings about Christ and be taken forward to maturity. Our citizenship requires us to learn the culture, the laws, the rights and privileges, etc., of our new country. The Holy Spirit is called the *parakletos*, the one who comes alongside of us because He lives in us (Luke 17:21). He is our help in the earth realm. Think about this: if Jesus had remained on the earth, He would only have been able to reach those within his physical geography. There was no technology to support His global mission until He ascended and turned it over to His Spirit to handle. So now help has come to every believer. But we must invoke the Spirit to help us.

Here is an example. It's like a wife who comes home from grocery shopping and enters her house having multiple bags of groceries in the car. Once she opens the door, she sees her three teenage children and husband sitting in the living room. They all hear her enter and turn and say, "Hey, Mom, we're glad you're back, we're hungry". She does not answer; she lays several bags of groceries on the counter and goes back out to the garage. She comes back in with her hands full and finds her children and spouse looking through the bags on the counter. She goes out a third time and comes back in to see that they have all grabbed some snacks and gone back to what they were doing. She knows she has one more trip to the car to get the last of the groceries. This time, she slams the garage door when she comes back in and says, "I cannot believe you all!" Her family turns around and says, "What?" She says, "You all saw me carrying in all these groceries, and not one of you came to help me or asked me if I needed any help." Their reply was, "Well, if you needed help, you should have asked." Her family, just like the Holy Spirit, is here to help. The Holy Spirit, like Jesus, will never intrude but waits to be invited.

Medical examination

In the world system, there are doctors in place to aid humans in monitoring our health needs. They base all their decisions on a set of circumstances occurring in one's body. Their diagnosis is not exact science, but they have tools to get as close as they can to treat whatever ailments are occurring. It is fascinating that man can donate body parts that can be reused in reconstructive surgeries, and that man has learned how to construct body parts from non-human parts to rebuild limbs, etc. However, there is one thing that medical science cannot do, and that is re-create blood for the human body. Blood has to come from another human donor.

In the kingdom, the blood that was shed on the cross by Jesus is the blood type of the citizens. As we are the offspring of Christ

Jesus, at the time of our acknowledgment of Jesus as Lord, a spiritual blood transfusion occurred that cleansed us from the contamination of sin and made us whole, clean, and healed (Isaiah 53:4-5; 1 John 1:7). So there is no need to check blood types, no need for further blood transfusions, no need to find donors, as His blood is sufficient. Regarding our other biometric data, there is no need to present our fingerprints or eye scans, no need for facial recognition, as our spiritual data is all inherent in Christ.

Having completed all of these worldly naturalization requirements makes one a new citizen in this natural world. The applicant can now attend their naturalization ceremony, have their certificate signed by the officials of the country, and receive the applicable government seal declaring that they are a citizen. In contrast, with the kingdom of God, our ceremony is declared officially received when we are born again with water and fire. All the work has been paid for and completed through Jesus' death, burial, and resurrection. The summation of our citizenship will be confirmed at the judgment seat of Christ.

CHAPTER 8

POWER FOR THE FUTURE

Being in and not immersed

With our citizenship accepted, and Jesus having left the planet, the deposit of the Holy Spirit must become activated within us. His residency means He lives in us every day. He does not disappear. He does not depart, He does not lift His presence from us. He remains. We must develop our relationship with Him to begin the process of conversion. Therefore, we need to submit to His authority as our teacher for the work in us that has yet to be done. With one of his roles being that of a teacher, I don't want to assume we understand what that means. A teacher is defined in the scriptures as one who "hold[s] discourse with others in order to instruct them."[13] Being a teacher implies relationship. Like having a virtual class where the speaker is not visible but is providing instruction via technology, the tool we have at our disposal is called prayer. The great thing about His classes is that we have access to Him 24/7. So, we must create a spiritual relationship with Him, just like the disciples did when they walked with Jesus. Just as they had questions for Jesus, we have the Holy Spirit to go to and get His mind on the matter we want to discuss.

We must remember that we are supernatural citizens of God's invisible kingdom, so being able to talk and speak to Him should not be strange to us. We have to come out of our natural mind into His supernatural kingdom to cultivate our relationship. God has done His part by sending His gift of the Spirit to us, and now it is up to us to receive Him. We should not assume that because He lives in us, we have received or opened our communication with Him. Just think of all the people you know who are living in a house with others they do not communicate with. As I stated before, a gift is not a gift until it is opened and received.

From promise to power

In order to fulfil our assignment in the earth, we need to receive the power of the Holy Spirit. This activation empowers us to take the pressure off of ourselves and place it on Him. His power untapped or unrestrained can be very detrimental to its work in our life. If it is untapped, we will never know the true potential and capabilities we have been given. If it is tapped with no restraint or accountability, great damage will occur to us and others, damaging the kingdom and its reputation. This is why we need to receive and open this gift, as He will then be able to guide us in pursuit of our kingdom life, not our own personal pursuits. Honestly,, God is not concerned with what we want to do. Remember the words in the Lord's Prayer: *"thy kingdom come, thy will be done on earth as it is in heaven."* This receipt of this power is an enablement for man to do what he could not do in his own strength. So, our reception of Him in our lives is paramount. If we don't receive Him, then we are rejecting His authority, and our God-ordained purpose will not be fulfilled. If we don't receive Him as the Spirit of truth, then we become renegades or bastards, illegitimate children (Hebrews 12:8).

Receiving is our responsibility. As we know, a person cannot receive if their hands or heart is already full of something else. We must release our grip on the old and allow our heart to be opened for reconstructive surgery. This release and exchange makes His spiritual power available to us. As the scripture says, His strength is made perfect in our weakness (2 Corinthians 12:9). This power helps us walk right, live right, love right, and give right according to the government of the kingdom of God. The concept of power like love has been so distorted in the world that we have accepted power as a personal need to obtain in order to lord over people rather than to help others and extend the kingdom of God. We can accredit this distortion to our captor, as his main job is to create doubt and disbelief in our relationship with God and to make everything about us and not Him.

This power we are speaking of came through a promise from Jesus to His disciples. When someone makes us a promise, if we trust the person who spoke the promise, then we can bank on the fact that they will do what they said. Jesus told His disciples after His resurrection to wait for the promise in Jerusalem that would come from the Father after His departure (Luke 24:49). That promise coincides with what He also spoke in John 14:26, that the Father would send them a comforter in His absence to teach and guide them into all the truth He had previously spoken to them. He wanted to assure His disciples that after His departure, they would not be alone, and that they would soon have that same power within them to operate, as He did as He spoke in John 14:12: *"Verily, verily, I say unto you, He that believeth on me, the works that I do shall he do also; and greater works than these shall he do; because I go unto my Father."*

Citizens of heaven, this clearly shows us that the power of the Holy Spirit is for all citizens of the kingdom, then and now. God has not changed His mind. The earth can only be transformed by His citizens through His way. The kingdom must become visible and tangible in the earth, and we are the ones to demonstrate that. Trust what the Bible says. Jesus' words that I cited here don't require reinterpretation; He was very clear. In Mark 16:17-18, Jesus said, *"And these signs shall follow them that believe; in my name they shall cast out devils; they shall speak with new tongues; They shall take up serpents; and if they drink any deadly thing, it shall not hurt them; they shall lay hands on the sick and they shall recover."* These activities are for His citizens.

When you go back and study these scriptures, you will find that these words were spoken before His final ascension to heaven. I liken this to when parents plan to go away for a short trip and tell the children their expectation of the chores to be completed before they come back. As the time for the trip comes closer, the parents reinforce their directives, hoping to embed their expectations into the minds of the children. When the day arrives, the parents do not take a chance and assume the children will remember, so they may write it down and/or reinforce through a family meeting to ensure everyone understood the assignment, as they wanted everything to be in order when they returned. This is what Jesus did in these scriptures. He made His wishes known regarding what was to happen when He went away. These instructions were His last words, which should not be dismissed as a suggestion, as He is reinforcing the plan of the Father through the Holy Spirit to fulfil His purpose.

Now we have clarity that there is power and a promise coming. This promise carries the power that every citizen will need to complete God's plan in the earth realm. As humans in this world, daily we feel inadequate, stressed, weak, powerless to make changes, and defeated, and often we don't have the strength to put in any extra time to the things that are important to our relationship with Jesus. This is what the power of the promise will do for us. When we connect to Him, we will receive supernatural capability to withstand everything that comes up against us. We will see the world with new eyes and know that nothing is impossible for us. Think of it this way: if you have a light in the room and it is not plugged into the source, the light will never receive the power to shine.

Heavenly messaging or power to live

Getting hooked up to the power source is the next phase. Moving from the promise to get to the power requires our faith. Hebrews 11:1 tells us that *"faith is the substance of things hoped for, the evidence of things not seen,"* meaning we pull down the things from the unseen realm into the seen realm. How? Because we are now connected to a supernatural realm that is activated through our faith (Full Assurance in the Holy Ghost). Anything from heaven is not supposed to make sense to our natural mind; it is a different country with a different language and operation. Our natural minds have been contaminated by our former captor. Through faith, we must receive the power of the Holy Spirit so we can complete the conversion of our soul, having our minds renewed with the kingdom operation. So, let's look at this promise of power the disciples were waiting on.

We know that the book of Acts is the blueprint of the church. The Apostles were the examples of the Holy Spirit's embodiment of power within them to extend and expand the kingdom of God on the earth. However, they just did not jump out and start doing the work of the ministry. The instructions they received from Jesus in Luke 24:49 were reconfirmed in Acts 1:4-5, to wait for the promise: *"And, being assembled together with them, commanded them that they should not depart from Jerusalem, but wait for the promise of the Father, which, saith he, ye have heard of me. For John truly baptized with water; but ye shall be baptized with the Holy Ghost not many days hence."* Let's stop for a minute to talk about baptism. The word baptism comes from the Greek word *baptizō* which means emersion. The initial baptism that John preached was a cleansing, a washing off of a watery grave and a rising up into a new life. We see shadows of this from the Old Testament when Moses went through the Red Sea and Joshua crossing over the river Jordan. In the New Testament the baptism that Jesus spoke of included more. What Jesus is referencing in the above scripture would be construed as an additional baptism for those citizens of the Old Testament, but what He was implying was after His resurrection baptism would represent the emersion of the citizen with water and fire, just as he told Nicodemus. Water and fire both purifying agents and become a necessary component for man to be able to fulfil his mission in the earth. More will be discussed in a later chapter.

Just to bring more clarity regarding this power, the Greek word for power in the scripture referenced above in Acts is *dunamis*, which is where we get the word "dynamite." In action, we know that dynamite has the power to change the configuration of anything. Here Jesus is talking about supernatural power that transcends human capabilities. The source of this power comes from heaven. Once received, it becomes strength, authority, and ability. If we as kingdom citizens are going to pursue Jesus' mandate to go into all the world, He knows we must have more than a great attitude, passion, or commitment to our assignment. This power will be the pivot of our citizenship of the kingdom. We must realize that there are opposing forces in the earth that will do anything to stop God's plan. We need all the arsenal the Holy Spirit has to offer to ensure our victory. Remembering that Psalm 155:16 tells us that God gave the earth to the children of men, it is our responsibility to rule the earth with our delegated authority.

Our spiritual enablement

Enablement is defined as "the action or process of providing individuals or entities with the means to do something."[14] The baptism of the Holy Spirit is this enablement. Jesus knew a transfer of power to his citizens was necessary to supply them with the capability to do the works he did in the earth. He gave us grace, that does not cover sin or replace the law, but an empowerment for His citizens to keep the law so we can do the greater works

He accomplished in the earth through and by His Spirit. The Apostles and others totalling 120 people went to Jerusalem as requested and waited for the promise after Jesus' resurrection. The promise showed up as a flaming fire upon all of them and they spoke in tongues: *"And they were all filled with the Holy Ghost, and began to speak with other tongues, as the Spirit gave them utterance"* (Acts 2:4). Speaking in tongues is one of most controversial of the many gifts that the Holy Spirit administered. I want to make note here for your consideration, that this was the first gift the Holy Spirit administered to the 120 in the upper room once Jesus ascended.

Communication is a vital organ in connecting and uniting people. Without it, it is difficult to bring people together for instruction. In a war, the first tactic the enemy uses is to disconnect, destroy, cut off, cripple, dismantle, and/or demolish the opponent's communication devices. If communication devices go down, the enemy can isolate and separate their opponent and bring them into captivity. God put the Holy Spirit in the earth as an anti-hacking measure so that the communication between the home country and His citizens would never be shut down. He can maneuverer His citizens to exercise their dominion in the earth. (See appendix VII for more scriptural references.)

Through activating the power of the baptism of the Spirit, we are never disconnected from our King; we always have access to Him. Also, this communication is impenetrable in the spirit realm and cannot be hacked. You may say, "Why do I need this gift when I can pray myself?" My response is, how can you hear from heaven if you are not on the kingdom citizen channel? Let me put it this way. People go to psychics, and the psychics tell them they are making contact with the spirit world to get you the answers you need. The psychics know that the spiritual realm is real, and their patrons walk away believing their messages. If one can believe that their words are true, then how much more should the citizens of heaven make spiritual communication with their home country and receive divine interpretation?

Some of you have been told that speaking in tongues was for the Apostles only and is no longer required today. This has been termed cessation. If that were true, then why do the scriptures say there were 120 people in the upper room in Acts 2:1-4? All 120 of those people were not Apostles. Scripture says in 2 Timothy 3:16-17, *"All Scripture is breathed out by God and profitable for teaching, for reproof, for correction, and for training in righteousness, that the man of God may be complete, equipped for every good work."* God's goal was to grant us His children delegated authority to rule the earth in His stead.

I am not going to go into the details of the distinction between speaking in a known or unknown language. That argument is a distraction that attempts to diminish the supernatural power that is granted to us to communicate with our heavenly headquarters. Satan is the author of confusion, and I believe that this enablement to speak in tongues, utilizing our heavenly language, is instrumental to keep our two-way communication open with heaven, our home country. Additionally, with Jesus having told Nicodemus that we must be born again to enter this new kingdom, why would a new language be inappropriate? When a child is born, it is not born with the language of its parents. A child learns to speak from listening to their parent. There must be a communication channel that goes beyond our earthly realm, because we are now connected to a country/kingdom that is not of this world. So when we are "born again" as the scriptures, there is a sound from our heavenly Father that we are to listen for which He divinely gives us so that we can communicate with Him. The truth is that we are supernatural creatures having a human experience in this natural world. We live in the earth, but we are not from here (Ephesians 1:4).

As a citizen of the kingdom, we built our faith on the confession of believing in a man (Jesus) we have never seen, who is coming back to take us to a place we have never been. This was our first act of faith. That act of faith set that spiritual precedent for everything else in our spiritual life to come. Remember, faith is the currency of heaven, it is all supernatural. When we try to use our best thinking to make our faith make sense, we always stop short of all that God has planned for us. I say all this to make the point that when we enter the kingdom, we learn to speak and understand the home country's language, as that was our original language that was taken away from us when Adam transgressed.

Think about what happened during the time of the Tower of Babel (Genesis 11:1-9). The Bible said the earth was all of one language and because of that, nothing was restrained for them to accomplish. As the record goes, the Godhead visited the earth and confounded their language so they could not complete what they set out to do. From there, He dispersed the people from the area, and multiple languages and cultures were created. What God used to disconnect man, in the book of Acts He now uses to unite man again. You say well when they spoke in tongues in the book of Acts they spoke in other cultures languages that those people understood. Yes, that is correct, which demonstrated the miraculous the power of the Holy Spirit to grant the Apostles this ability to speak in another language right in front of non believers that represented many countries. From there the Apostles took the gospel to the Jews and Gentiles and at the time of physical baptism, the burial of the old life and the resurrection of their new life in Christ would be represented with a new language which would be the unifying connection of all future believers to their home country, heaven. This time, unification would be under the power and influence of the Holy Spirit. See appendix VII for more detailed information.

Ambassadors

This unification of the kingdom feeds right into the role of the citizens, who are also called ambassadors. The Apostle Paul tells us in 1 Corinthians 5:20 (AMP), *"So we are ambassadors for Christ, as though God were making His appeal through us; we [as Christ's representatives] plead with you on behalf of Christ to be reconciled to God."* An ambassador is one who acts as an agent or representative of their home country. These representatives speak on behalf of their government's interest and use their diplomacy to foster relationships with other countries as well as navigate worldwide challenges that impact multiple nations. This is where communication from the home country becomes critical. Since the home country/government oversees our lives, it is critical to be a part of the daily communications to get their mind on what is happening in the territories.

We are witnessing constant upheaval across the world at a rate never seen before: violence breaking out everywhere, disasters, famines, government coups, financial systems breaking down, cyber attacks, and assassinations. The daily briefing from the Holy Spirit keeps the ambassadors alert to prepare for what is to come, be it peace or war, ensuring that their life, family, and embassy have the appropriate instructions.

The Holy Spirit is responsible for ensuring that the ambassadors operate in the accepted manner, following the customs and cultural behavior's mandated by the home country. He trains them in how to communicate in their assigned territory. The first order for the ambassadors to learn is that they have no opinion. They can only speak using the messaging that has come down from their home country. They do not negotiate with their home country. The Holy Spirit holds daily calls with them to disseminate the required information. This ensures that no matter where the ambassadors are deployed, they are equipped on all foreign-affairs matters that require immediate attention. However, it is the responsibility of the ambassador to initiate communication to the home country if there is an assault on their person, their family, or the embassy, as the home country will intervene to provide safety, shelter and direction concerning them. During the ambassador's appointment to their territory, they are supplied living quarters, food, clothing, and protection. They don't have to pay for anything. Their assignment is totally covered by the home country, and their residency is permanent unless they are recalled or redeployed to another region as the home country requires.

In our capacity as ambassadors, the diplomatic role in which we are to engage in our assigned territory is to lead foreigners into reconciliation to God. After we came out of enslavement by our captor, our previous manners, culture, communication, allegiance, and compliance were not of a diplomatic nature. We cannot become effective ambassadors if we don't submit to the Holy Spirit's training and guidance that is in compliance with the example Jesus set on earth for us. Since our job is to spread the influence of our government to all foreigners, we should desire to be like the Apostle Paul, who said in Ephesians 6:18-20,

> *Praying always with all prayer and supplication in the Spirit, and watching thereunto with all perseverance and supplication for all saints; And for me, that utterance may be given unto me, that I may open my mouth boldly, to make known. the mystery of the gospel, For which I am an ambassador in bonds: that therein I may speak boldly, as I ought to speak.*

In a true kingdom structure, we live by the king's orders, and we have no opinions. We don't negotiate with the king. As I just said, this is a foreign concept to those in a democratic republic, because our constitution tells us we can vote leaders in and out, we have free speech, and the list goes on. All of these rights are contrary to how a kingdom is ruled by a sovereign God. The Holy Spirit's goal is to duplicate the home country's language, values, characteristics, and culture, whereas our responsibility as citizens in our ambassador role is to carry and promote the King's agenda.

CONCLUSION

Becoming a Citizen of the Kingdom

The Bible was not written to be like every other book. It is the constitution of heaven where all mankind originated. That being said, we need to know all our rights, our privileges, and the laws that govern our new kingdom. We must shed these old grave clothes that were given to us by our captor and be freed from the spiritual Stockholm Syndrome we were enslaved to at our natural birth. With our eyes open now to the reason God created man, we can see that the Bible is not only a book to be read and quoted, rather to be read to understand the author and His intentions. It is not a rule book, but a guidebook. It provides us with direction, correction, and instruction for everything pertaining to life. Once we receive the full counsel of the kingdom of God, we will learn how to walk right, live right, and love right. We all carry an individual responsibility to living it, and we will one day have to answer to that. We should never be wise in our own eyes to think we have the full understanding of who God is. The scripture tells us that all the things He ever did and said could not be contained in the book (John 21:25). Reading the scriptures is just the first step; revelation comes by the Holy Spirit. He is the author of life. We must be careful to know that it is easy to misplace our own thoughts and emotions over His desires. As citizens of His kingdom, it is imperative that we understand that in a kingdom, whatever the King speaks becomes law, and the citizens do not get the opportunity to come to His table to voice our opinions. Remember that He created us for Him and not Him for us. Yes, He is there for His citizens, but solely in the context of fulfilling His purpose for the Kingdom He was creating.

Getting another perspective will bring more depth to our understanding. It is easy to maintain our limited views and opinions of the way we were indoctrinated into something. The beauty about perspective is that you keep your eyes on the focal point but utilize different vantage points to ensure that you are seeing accurately. From my perspective, the church does not lack truth, but rather the application of His truth. If the church is so right, then why are we not seeing the power and transformation? There are fewer and fewer people going to church today than ever before. We can blame it on the end times, but I believe it is because we need to tweak our messaging to align with what Jesus preached. As I said earlier, our sermons are focused on what we can get from God rather than what we can give. This may not be your church, but the attendance does not lie. God bless all those who have gone before us in teaching this gospel of the kingdom, but now it is our responsibility to continue to move His message forward.

Conclusion

The earthly concept of Stockholm Syndrome equates to mankind's relationship with our captor, Satan. We are born into the earth with a sin nature, and this automatically, without our choice, gave us a new constitution to follow. That constitution gave us a sentence of eternal death and exposure to sickness and disease, with a built-in anti-God mindset, independent disposition, and a self-made-man classification. This captivity keeps man blinded to his original Creator and our true inheritance. But God sent Jesus to come down from heaven to rescue us from our spiritual ignorance, as we could not opt out of the eternal judgment death had over us. We were powerless to alter that constitution within ourselves.

There is a saying most have heard: "If you don't know your history, you are destined to repeat it." Without truly understanding our history, we set ourselves up to live in a false narrative about our lives and how they began and how it will end. When we talk to people, everyone has a story of their beginnings, but I find it interesting that everyone's narrative starts with themselves as if they do not have a creator, even if it is not the God we serve through Jesus Christ. The whole world is searching for the kingdom. Every religion is seeking an eternal resting place; every religion is seeking a leader or some form of deity to take responsibility over them AMP Luke 16:16), The Law and the [writings of the] Prophets were proclaimed until John; since then the gospel of the kingdom of God has been *and* continues to be preached, and everyone tries forcefully to go into it. This means there is obviously something innately within man that is searching for more. I believe that something comes from the breath God breathing into man to make him a living soul. That

Conclusion

breath is apart of all men despite their acknowledgement of Jesus. That is why Jesus died for all humanity to end that search by bringing His kingdom to the earth. If Adam had never sinned, all of humanity would be operating with the kingdom of God mindset, which would have negated the need for religion, and that includes Christianity. The prophets preached the kingdom, John the Baptist preached the kingdom, Jesus preached the kingdom, the Apostles preached the kingdom, and the Holy Spirit was the regenerative force that guided us into the kingdom. No where was religion apart of what the bible teaches.

I pray you find this perspective illuminating to the knowledge you currently possess while being prompted to revisit this message to be sure you are in alignment with our King. Hopefully with this revelation, you can see the impacts that Satan had on our lives, and how the need to understand the gospel of the kingdom feeds into God's overall intention for man.

I have been in the ministry now for over 25 years, and I am still uncovering the mysteries of scripture. I had never been content to hold on to what I have been told by faith. It was not because I was critical or unbelieving. I know that faith implies that one would never have all the answers, but one thing I did know was that there were more answers to be found than what I heard on Sunday morning. I wanted to understand how the devil got on the earth. I wanted to know when hell was created. I wanted to understand where and how evil came into being. I wanted to know why Adam never asked to come back into the garden. I wanted to know what Jesus set me free from, because I did not believe I was ever in bondage to anyone. What I have learned

Conclusion

is that I had to go to God with these hard questions that were never answered from the pulpits I had been in.

Once we accept that we are a people who were spiritually kidnapped and raised by the first identity thief, we will recognize that we have never known our true spiritual identity.

It's like going to a new medical doctor. They ask you to fill out a sheet that asks about your family's medical history of illnesses: stroke, heart disease, cancer, etc. They do this because natural medicine has found that through your DNA, there is coding inherited from your biological parents that was passed down and possesses a higher propensity to produce those same illnesses in you. It allows your medical providers to take proactive testing, in hopes of intercepting those same sicknesses and diseases from coming upon you. When you don't know your family's medical history, it complicates obtaining an accurate diagnosis, which makes you subject to random tests, medications, and unnecessary costs to properly diagnose you. Just as in the natural, a family's medical history is good to know, so it is with our spiritual history.

Our spiritual history from the Bible tells us we were initially encoded with God's DNA that was pure and untainted—a genetic code that would cause us to live eternally. However, there came a point when our ancestors picked up a virus that brought physical death to us, which separated us from our Father. The doctors, knowing this history, advised us that the only way we could live eternally would be to have someone donate their blood so the life force in us could rule over the deadly virus and we could live and be free from it.

After salvation, the Holy Spirit's job is to show us how to live now that we have been set free from that infectious disease that was designed to kill us eternally. His role in our lives is to show us how to use this freedom to fulfil the original purpose God had intended in the earth. The blood of Jesus has cleansed us of our sin, but the Holy Ghost is here to help us kill the viruses that still contaminates our soul. Through our submission to His power, we will are reborn, restored, renewed, and reconciled to recover all that was lost from the garden through Adam. Becoming a walking example of the gospel of the kingdom, loosing ourselves from the philosophies and thoughts of this world and adopting righteous principles that were established to govern us by protecting and sustaining us until our assignment is complete in the earth.

So, what shall we say to these things? We must know that our God is so awesome that He continues to reveal Himself to His creation. We must be able to distinguish between God's word, our world, and the world's attempts to dismantle God's operation in the earth. Before we criticize or dismiss understanding God's world, purpose. and plan, we should dig a little deeper into the Bible to investigate. Joshua told us to meditate on the word; Timothy told us to study the word; Paul told us to renew our minds; and Jesus told us to ask, seek, and knock. Those directives were not aimed at or limited to leaders alone; they were meant for all citizens of His kingdom. Why? Because God wants to be known and understood.

It was and is always God's intent to reveal himself to His children. It is not acceptable to be like the people of the Old Testament who looked for the leaders of the day to be their spokespeople for God, looking for those leaders to walk ahead of them and shield them from the dangers they would come across. That time was to demonstrate that God was with them,

Conclusion

but now He has put His Spirit in us so that we can know as individuals that He is with us to guide and teach us along the way. This is how relationships and revelation are achieved. We have a responsibility to the Father.

Humans have a tendency to see only what we want to see. God is not obligated to reveal Himself to those who are not seeking Him. He has the answers to our questions, but we have to engage with Him even in our scepticism. Keep in mind that when the disciples walked with Jesus, they did not understand everything He did or why things happened, and yet they believed. We can rest assured that when we seek Him, we will find Him, and He will make Himself known to us. He gave us that promise. It is my prayer that you use this book as a tool to enhance your journey with the Lord to bring us all together in the unity of the faith.

What I have attempted to do in this book is to pass along the revelation God gave me about His world, His purpose, and His plan. To reveal the scriptures from His perspective, in which He extends His kingdom from heaven to earth, giving His creation authority to rule and reign just as He does in heaven. He assigned His royal family to help facilitate this process and will return when it is completed. If we want to know when the end will come, he tells us in Matthew 24:14 *And **this gospel of the kingdom shall be preached** in all the world for a witness unto all nations; **and then shall the end come**.* We have work to do, let get at it!

Conclusion

But without faith it is impossible to please him: for he that cometh to God must believe that he is, and that he is a rewarder of them that diligently seek him.

Hebrews 11:6

Appendix

In this appendix, I have included scriptural references in support of the subject matter discussed. It is not meant to be an exhaustive list but to highlight the important scriptures as a quick guide to aid you to pursue further study.

I. **Scriptures supporting things that were completed in God's eternal world BEFORE the earth was created. Knowing these scriptures and looking up the definitions of the highlighted words will change your perspective on how you read the bible.**

   God ordained us to walk in good works before creation

   Ephesians 2:10 *For we are his workmanship, created in Christ Jesus unto good works, which God hath **before ordained** that we should walk in them.*

   Jesus was with God in the beginning

   Proverbs 8:23-24 *I was set up **from everlasting**, from the beginning, or ever the earth was. When there were no depths, I was brought forth; when there were no fountains abounding with water.*

Appendix

Jesus already knows who will make it into heaven

Revelation 17:8 *The beast that thou sawest was, and is not; and shall ascend out of the bottomless pit, and go into perdition: and they that dwell on the earth shall wonder, whose names were not written in the book of life **from the foundation of the world**, when they behold the beast that was, and is not, and yet is.*

Jesus was slain before the earth was created

Revelation 13:8 *And all that dwell upon the earth shall worship him, whose names are not written in the book of life of **the Lamb slain from the foundation of the world**.*

Mankind predated the earth and was given purpose

2 Timothy 1:9 *Who hath saved us, and called us with an holy calling, not according to our works, but according to his own purpose and grace, which was given us in Christ Jesus **before the world began**.*

Ephesians 1:4 *According as **he hath chosen us in him before the foundation of the world**, that we should be holy and without blame before him in love.*

God declared everything that would happen before He created the earth

Isaiah 46:10 *Declaring the end from the beginning, and **from ancient times the things that are not yet done**, saying, My counsel shall stand, and I will do all my pleasure.*

Jesus knew before the foundation of the world what was to occur and what He would have to do

Appendix

1 Peter 1:19-20 *But with the precious blood of Christ, as of the lamb without blemish and without spot: Who verily was **foreordained before the foundation of the world**, but was manifest in these last times for you.*

Acts 4:27-28 *For of a truth against thy holy child Jesus, whom thou hast anointed, both Herod, and Pontius Pilate, with the Gentiles, and the people of Israel, were gathered together, For to do whatsoever thy hand and thy counsel **determined before** to be done.*

The devil sinned before the earth was created

1 John 3:8 *He that committeth sin is of the devil; for the devil sinneth **from the beginning**. For this purpose the Son of God was manifested, that he might destroy the works of the devil.*

The devil was a liar from the beginning

John 8:44 *Ye are of your father the devil, and the lusts of your father ye will do. He was **a murderer from the beginning**, and abode not in the truth, because there is no truth in him. When he speaketh a lie, he speaketh of his own: for he is a liar, and the father of it.*

Jesus knew Judas would betray him

John 6:64 *But there are some of you that believe not. For Jesus knew **from the beginning** who they were that believed not, and who should betray him.*

Divorce was never God's will

Matthew 19:8 *He saith unto them, Moses because of the hardness of your hearts suffered you to put away your wives: but **from the beginning** it was not so.*

All humanity was chosen in Christ before the earth was created

Ephesians 1:4 *According as **he hath chosen us in him before the foundation of the world**, that we should be holy and without blame before him in love.*

Everything in the unseen realm was created by God

Romans 1:20 *For the invisible things of him **from the creation of the world** are clearly seen, being understood by the things that are made, even his eternal power and Godhead; so that they are without excuse.*

Affliction will come to the earth like never before

Mark 13:19 *For in those days shall be affliction, such as was not **from the beginning** of the creation which God created unto this time, neither shall be.*

God hid the wisdom of His plans in the beginning

1 Corinthians 2:7 *But we speak the wisdom of God in a mystery, even the wisdom, which **God ordained before the world unto our glory**.*

Mankind was predestined with an inheritance

Ephesians 1:11 *In whom also we have obtained an inheritance, **being predestinated according to the purpose of him** who worketh all things after the counsel of his own will.*

APPENDIX

Jesus was glorified in heaven with the Father

> **John 17:5** *And now, O Father, glorify thou me with thine own self with the glory which I had with thee **before the world was**.*

II. **Scriptures that support man's captivity, i.e. under Satan's rule, the kingdom of darkness, i.e. (Spiritual Stockholm Syndrome)**

> **John 8:12** *Then spake Jesus again unto them, saying, I am the light of the world: **he that followeth me shall not walk in darkness**, but shall have the light of life.*
>
> **John 12:46** *I am come a light into the world, that **whosoever believeth on me should not abide in darkness**.*
>
> **2 Corinthians 4:4** *In whom **the god of this world hath blinded the minds of them which believe not,** lest the light of the glorious gospel of Christ, who is the image of God, should shine unto them.*
>
> **Acts 26:18** ***To open their eyes, and to turn them from darkness to light**, and from the power of Satan unto God, that they may receive forgiveness of sins, and inheritance among them which are sanctified by faith that is in me.*
>
> **Ephesians 5:8** ***For ye were sometimes darkness**, but now are ye light in the Lord: walk as children of light.*
>
> **Colossians 1:13** *Who hath **delivered us from the power of darkness**, and hath translated us into the kingdom of his dear Son.*
>
> **1 Peter 2:9** *But ye are a chosen generation, a royal priesthood, an holy nation, a peculiar people; that ye should shew forth*

the praises of him **who hath called you out of darkness into his marvellous light.**

2 Timothy 2:26 *And that they may* **recover themselves out of the snare of the devil, who are taken captive by him at his will.**

Psalm 18:28 *For thou wilt light my candle: the LORD my* **God will enlighten my darkness.**

Romans 6:6 *Knowing this, that our old man is crucified with him,* **that the body of sin might be destroyed,** *that henceforth we should not serve sin.*

Romans 8:21 *Because the creature itself also shall be* **delivered from the bondage of corruption** *into the glorious liberty of the children of God.*

III. **Scriptures supporting the importance God placed on children. The important factor here is that there is no extension of his kingdom if there are no offspring.**

Genesis 1:28 *And God blessed them, and God said unto them, Be fruitful, and* **multiply, and replenish the earth,** *and subdue it: and have dominion over the fish of the sea, and over the fowl of the air, and over every living thing that moveth upon the earth.*

Psalms 127:3 *Lo,* **children are an heritage** *of the Lord: and the fruit of the womb is his reward.*

Exodus 1:7 *And the children of Israel were fruitful, and* **increased abundantly, and multiplied, and waxed exceeding mighty;** *and the land was filled with them.*

Appendix

Psalm 115:16 *The heaven, even the heavens, are the Lord's: but **the earth hath he given to the children of men**.*

IV. Scriptures supporting the prophets speaking of the coming of the kingdom of God

Moses

Exodus 19:6 ***And ye shall be unto me a kingdom of priests, and an holy nation.*** *These are the words which thou shalt speak unto the children of Israel.*

Daniel

Daniel 2:44 *And in the days of these kings shall **the God of heaven set up a kingdom**, which shall never be destroyed: and the kingdom shall not be left to other people, but it shall break in pieces and consume all these kingdoms, and it shall stand for ever.*

Daniel 7:18 *But **the saints of the most High shall take the kingdom, and possess the kingdom forever**, even for ever and ever.*

Daniel 7:22 *Until the Ancient of days came, and judgment was given to the saints of the most High; and the time came that **the saints possessed the kingdom**.*

Daniel 7:27 *And the kingdom and dominion, and the greatness of **the kingdom under the whole heaven, shall be given to the people of the saints of the most High**, whose kingdom is an everlasting kingdom, and all dominions shall serve and obey him.*

Samuel

1 Samuel 10:25 *Then **Samuel told the people the manner of the kingdom**, and wrote it in a book, and laid it up before the Lord. And Samuel sent all the people away, every man to his house.*

1 Samuel 11:14 *Then said Samuel to the people,* **Come, and let us go to Gilgal, and renew the kingdom there.**

Isaiah

Isaiah 9:6 *For unto us a child is born, unto us a son is given: and* **the government shall be upon his shoulder:** *and his name shall be called Wonderful, Counsellor, The mighty God, The everlasting Father, The Prince of Peace.*

David

Psalms 103:19 *The Lord hath prepared his throne in the heavens; and* **his kingdom ruleth over all.**

V. Scriptures supporting Jesus preaching the gospel of the kingdom of God

Matthew 4:17 *From that time* ***Jesus began to preach, and to say, Repent: for the kingdom of heaven is at hand.***

Matthew 4:23 *And Jesus went about all Galilee, teaching in their synagogues, and* **preaching the gospel of the kingdom**, *and healing all manner of sickness and all manner of disease among the people.*

Matthew 9:35 *And Jesus went about all the cities and villages, teaching in their synagogues, and* **preaching the gospel of the kingdom**, *and healing every sickness and every disease among the people.*

Mark 1:14 *Now after that John was put in prison, Jesus came into Galilee,* **preaching the gospel of the kingdom** *of God.*

Luke 9:11 *And the people, when they knew it, followed him: and he received them, and* **spake unto them of the kingdom of God***, and healed them that had need of healing.*

Luke 8:1 *And it came to pass afterward, that he went throughout every city and village, preaching and* **shewing the glad tidings of the kingdom** *of God: and the twelve were with him.*

Acts 1:2-3 *Until the day in which he was taken up, after that he through the Holy Ghost had given commandments unto the apostles whom he had chosen: To whom also he shewed himself alive after his passion by many infallible proofs, being seen of them forty days, and* **speaking of the things pertaining to the kingdom of God.**

Matthew 24:14 *And* **this gospel of the kingdom** *shall be preached in all the world for a witness unto all nations; and then shall the end come.*

VI. Scriptures supporting the Apostles expansion of the preaching of the gospel of the kingdom

Phillip preaching in Samaria

Acts 8:12 *But when they believed Philip* **preaching the things concerning the kingdom** *of God, and the name of Jesus Christ, they were baptized, both men and women.*

Apostle Paul and Barnabas preaching in Derbe, Lystra and Iconium

Acts 14:20-22 *Howbeit, as the disciples stood round about him, he rose up, and came into the city: and the next day he departed with Barnabas to Derbe.[21] And when they had preached the gospel to that city, and had taught many, they returned again to Lystra, and to Iconium, and Antioch,[22] Confirming the souls of the disciples, and **exhorting them to continue in the faith, and that we must through much tribulation enter into the kingdom of God.***

Apostle Paul preaching in Ephesus

Acts 19:8 *And he went into the synagogue, and spake boldly for the space of three months, **disputing and persuading the things concerning the kingdom of God.***

Apostle Paul with the elders of the church in Ephesus

Acts 20:25 *And now, behold, I know that ye all, among whom I have gone **preaching the kingdom** of God, shall see my face no more.*

Apostle Paul speaking to the Jews in Rome

Acts 28:31 ***Preaching the kingdom of God,** and teaching those things which concern the Lord Jesus Christ, with all confidence, no man forbidding him.*

VII. **Scriptural support that the baptism of the Holy Spirit with the evidence of speaking in tongues was the power given to the Apostles which they received in the upper room and extended to those who were baptised as they spread the gospel of the kingdom to the Jews and Gentiles.**

Appendix

The baptism of the Holy Ghost upon the 120 in the upper room after Jesus' ascension.

Acts 2:1-4 (ESV) *When the day of Pentecost arrived, they were all together in one place. And suddenly there came from heaven a sound like a mighty rushing wind, and it filled the entire house where they were sitting. And divided tongues as of fire appeared to them and rested on each one of them.* ***And they were all filled with the Holy Spirit and began to speak in other tongues as the Spirit gave them utterance.***

Apostle Peter speaking to a crowd of people from Judea and Jerusalem

Acts 2:37-39 *Now when they heard this, they were pricked in their heart, and said unto Peter and to the rest of the apostles, Men and brethren, what shall we do?* ^{38} *Then Peter said unto them, Repent, and be baptized every one of you in the name of Jesus Christ for the remission of sins,* ***and ye shall receive the gift of the Holy Ghost.*** ^{39} ***For the promise is unto you, and to your children***, *and to all that are afar off, even as many as the Lord our God shall call.*

Apostle Peter and John in Samaria baptizing believers in the Holy Spirit.

Acts 8:14-20 *Now when the apostles which were at Jerusalem heard that Samaria had received the word of God, they sent unto them Peter and John:* ^{15} *Who, when they were come down, prayed for them, that they might receive the Holy Ghost:* ^{16} *(For as yet he was fallen upon none of them:* ***only they were baptized in the name of the Lord Jesus.****)* ^{17} *Then laid they their hands on them, and they* *received the Holy Ghost.*¹⁸ *And **when Simon saw** that through laying on of the apostles' hands the Holy Ghost was given, he offered them money,*¹⁹ *Saying, Give me also this power, that on whomsoever I lay hands, he may receive the Holy Ghost.*²⁰ *But Peter said unto him, Thy money perish with thee, because thou hast thought that the gift of God may be purchased with money.*

Saul's conversion at Damascus

Acts 9:17 *And Ananias went his way, and entered into the house; and putting his hands on him said, Brother Saul, the Lord, even Jesus, that appeared unto thee in the way as thou camest, hath sent me,* **that thou mightest receive thy sight, and be filled with the Holy Ghost.**

The Apostle Peter in Caesarea talking with Cornelius and his friends

Acts 10:37-48 *That word, I say, ye know, which was published throughout all Judaea, and began from Galilee, after the baptism which John preached;*³⁸ *How God anointed Jesus of Nazareth with the Holy Ghost and with power: who went about doing good, and healing all that were oppressed of the devil; for God was with him.*³⁹ *And we are witnesses of all things which he did both in the land of the Jews, and in Jerusalem; whom they slew and hanged on a tree:*⁴⁰ *Him God raised up the third day, and shewed him openly;*⁴¹ *Not to all the people, but unto witnesses chosen before God, even to us, who did eat and drink with him after he rose from the dead.*⁴² *And he commanded us to preach unto the people, and to testify that it is he which was ordained of God to be the Judge of quick and dead.* ⁴³ *To him give all the prophets* *witness, that through his name whosoever believeth in him shall receive remission of sins.*[44] *While Peter yet spake these words, the Holy Ghost fell on all them which heard the word.*[45] *And they of the circumcision which believed were astonished, as many as came with Peter, because that on the Gentiles also was poured out the gift of the Holy Ghost.*[46] *For they heard them speak with tongues, and magnify God. Then answered Peter,*[47] *Can any man forbid water, that these should not be baptized, which have received the Holy Ghost as well as we?*[48] *And he commanded them to be baptized in the name of the Lord. Then prayed they him to tarry certain days.*

Apostle Paul in Ephesus inquiring to the disciples there if they have received the gift of the Holy Ghost.

Acts 19:2 *He said unto them, Have ye received the Holy Ghost since ye believed? And they said unto him, We have not so much as heard whether there be any Holy Ghost.* [3] *And he said unto them, Unto what then were ye baptized? And they said, Unto John's baptism.*[4] *Then said Paul, John verily baptized with the baptism of repentance, saying unto the people, that they should believe on him which should come after him, that is, on Christ Jesus.*[5] *When they heard this, they were baptized in the name of the Lord Jesus.*[6] *And when Paul had laid his hands upon them, the Holy Ghost came on them; and they spake with tongues, and prophesied.*[7] *And all the men were about twelve.*

Peter was in Jerusalem defending his time spent with the Gentiles and how they too received the baptism of the Holy Ghost.

Acts 11:15 *And as I began to speak, the Holy Ghost fell on them, as on us at the beginning.*

Jude the brother of Jesus telling others to pray in the Holy Spirit as He knows how to interpret God's will.

Jude 1:20 *But ye, beloved, building up yourselves on your most holy faith, praying in the Holy Ghost,*

VIII. Scriptures supporting the importance of God's precepts, His commands/laws that govern His kingdom. These are not the ritual laws of the Old Testament but His governing principles that rule over His kingdom that King David wrote about which made him a man after God's own heart.

Nehemiah 9:13-14 *You came down also on Mount Sinai, And spoke with them from heaven, And gave them just ordinances and true laws, Good statutes and commandments. ¹⁴ You made known to them Your holy Sabbath, And commanded them precepts, statutes and laws, By the hand of Moses Your servant.*

Psalm 119:4 *You have commanded us to keep Your precepts diligently.*

Psalm 119:15 *I will meditate in thy precepts, and have respect unto thy ways*

Psalm 119:27 *Make me to understand the way of thy precepts: so shall I talk of thy wondrous works.*

Psalm 119:40 *Behold, I have longed after thy precepts: quicken me in thy righteousness.*

APPENDIX

Psalm 119:45 *And I will walk at liberty: for I seek thy precepts.*

Psalm 119:56 *This I had, because I kept thy precepts.*

Psalm 119:63 *I am a companion of all them that fear thee, and of them that keep thy precepts.*

Psalm 119:69 *The proud have forged a lie against me: but I will keep thy precepts with my whole heart.*

Psalm 119:78 *Let the proud be ashamed; for they dealt perversely with me without a cause: but I will meditate in thy precepts.*

Psalm 119:87 *They had almost consumed me upon earth; but I forsook not thy precepts.*

Psalm 119:93 *I will never forget thy precepts: for with them thou hast quickened me.*

Psalm 119:94 *I am thine, save me: for I have sought thy precepts.*

Psalm 119:100 *I understand more than the ancients, because I keep thy precepts.*

Psalm 119:104 *Through thy precepts I get understanding: therefore I hate every false way.*

Psalm 119:110 *The wicked have laid a snare for me: yet I erred not from thy precepts.*

Psalm 119:128 *Therefore I esteem all thy precepts concerning all things to be right; and I hate every false way.*

Psalm 119:134 *Deliver me from the oppression of man: so will I keep thy precepts.*

Appendix

Psalm 119:141 *I am small and despised: yet do not I forget thy precepts.*

Psalm 119:159 *Consider how I love thy precepts: quicken me, O Lord, according to thy lovingkindness.*

Psalm 119:168 *I have kept thy precepts and thy testimonies: for all my ways are before thee.*

Psalm 119:173 *Let thine hand help me; for I have chosen thy precepts.*

Endnotes

1. https://www.investopedia.com/terms/e/estateplanning.asp
2. https://webstersdictionary1828.com/Dictionary/precept
3. https://en.wikipedia.org/wiki/Stockholm_syndrome#:~:text=Stockholm%20syndrome%20is%20a%20proposed,validity%20or%20useful%20sample%20size.
4. https://www.britannica.com/science/Stockholm-syndrome
5. https://www.healthline.com/health/womens-health/how-many-eggs-does-a-woman-have#how-many
6. https://ro.co/fertility/when-do-men-stop-producing-sperm/
7. Donavyn Coffey, "Why Does Christianity Have So Many Denominations?" LiveScience, July 29, 2022, https://www.livescience.com/christianity-denominations.html.
8. https://populationeducation.org/world-population-by-religion-a-global-tapestry-of-faith
9. Noah Webster, 1928 Webster's American Dictionary of the English Language, Pg 378

10. Myles Munroe, Kingdom Principles: Preparing for Kingdom Experience and Expansion (Destiny Image Publishers, 2006), 31.

11. https://www.blueletterbible.org/lexicon/g3340/kjv/tr/0-1/

12. https://www.blueletterbible.org/lexicon/g1994/kjv/tr/0-1/

13. https://www.blueletterbible.org/lexicon/g1321/kjv/tr/0-1/

14. https://www.vocabulary.com/dictionary/enablement

www.ingramcontent.com/pod-product-compliance
Lightning Source LLC
Chambersburg PA
CBHW062225080426
42734CB00010B/2035